"I have known Kevin for a long time. ⟨...⟩ctices for anyone wanting to stay competitive, ⟨...⟩ eir career but also in their life." —**Peyton Man**⟨...⟩

"In his debut book, *The Greatest S⟨...⟩ ⟨...⟩areer, and Transform Your Life*, songwriter/author Kevin Griffin delivers! It gives readers a real inside look at the craft and the industry. With its unique perspective on the art of songwriting, this book is a must-read for music enthusiasts and aspiring songwriters alike." —**Harvey Mason Jr., CEO of the Recording Academy / GRAMMY Awards, Songwriter, and Producer**

"This is a book for achievers. Those who want the edge to get ahead and stay there." —**Sean Payton, NFL Football Coach**

"*The Greatest Song* is inspired by one of the greatest success stories in the modern-day music business. They say truth is stranger than fiction, and Kevin combines the two, resulting in a thoroughly unique success story unlike any other in the music business—or any other business for that matter. A timeless tale of reinvention and creativity that applies to everyone in any career." —**Leslie Fram, Senior Vice President of Music Strategy for CMT**

"If you're looking for practical tools to both get you inspired and keep you motivated, this book is for you. If you love music and the air of songwriting, this book is for you!" —**Bobby Bones, Radio and TV Personality and *New York Times* Bestselling Author**

"An engaging read by Kevin Griffin, based on personal experience and dedicated to the notes in our lives. *The Greatest Song*, just like a great song, is written with interesting content and perfect cadence—telling a story *of* life and *for* life. Everyone in the music business should take the time to learn from, and enjoy, this read, before passing it on to someone you care about. My wife, Mary, and I picked it up to take our first dose of it and ended up finishing the whole prescription before putting it down. I just wish I had access to this work when I began my music career—I would have done some things much differently! Kevin explains the necessary steps to create your own successful personal and business life, using the tools of a beautifully written song to remind us that 'it's not what you take when you leave this world behind, it's what you leave behind when you go.'" —**Randy Travis, Seven-Time GRAMMY Award-Winning Recording Artist**

"I spent many years resisting collaborative songwriting, telling myself that I wrote my best songs when I wrote alone. And while that was true—I had quite a run of hits—the larger truth was that I feared cowriting. Through the years, I learned many of the lessons Kevin Griffin alludes to in his book . . . all the hard way! Although this book is technically fiction, the constructive ideas regarding the importance of listening and putting the song ahead of the ego can help young songwriters avoid some of the pitfalls that have taken me a career to understand. Plus, the main character, not unlike myself, proudly sports a man-purse!" —**Kevin Cronin, Lead Vocalist and Songwriter of REO Speedwagon**

"This is the one book to read about how to remain relevant in today's music industry. In *The Greatest Song*, Kevin masterfully develops the mindset of how to keep success in a constantly evolving business. His method demonstrates how thinking like a musician can provide valuable lessons for entrepreneurs and anyone who is trying to generate something new. This book is a must-read for those looking to boost innovation and inspire their creative journey, both personally and professionally." —**Panos A. Panay, President of the Recording Academy / GRAMMY Awards; Coauthor, *Two Beats Ahead: What Musical Minds Teach Us About Innovation***

"Kevin Griffin's book, *The Greatest Song: Spark Creativity, Ignite Your Career, and Transform Your Life*, is a must-read for everyone in all walks of life. It covers topics such as commitment, perseverance, evolution, and flexibility and adaptability to constantly changing circumstances that will help business leaders, entrepreneurs, musicians, and entertainers both professionally and personally. It's a timeless, inspirational story that will help you stay motivated and always ahead." —**Cesar Gueikian, President of Gibson Guitars**

"Man, I wish Kevin's book was around when I was younger—might've gotten more life out of these frosted tips! Great lessons not just for a career in music, but success in life . . . from one of our generation's finest songwriters." —**Mark McGrath, Singer and Songwriter for Sugar Ray**

"The wisdom here isn't just for musicians; it is for anyone who desires to find their best self within. Kevin's undeniable ability to communicate through song presents gem after gem of life and adaptable knowledge as expressed by a true master of his craft. But it's the human perspective of a father, a friend, an entrepreneur, and a true seeker that resonates. Kevin is that person who has always made everyone around him want to excel, and you will feel the same from this thoughtful and practical gift of a book." —**Jeff Rabhan, Chair Emeritus, Clive Davis Institute of Recorded Music at New York University**

"I've written some of my favorite songs with Kevin 'By-Tor' Griffin in the ten-plus years we've been working together. He always brings a sense of ambition, wonder, and humor to a writing session. His process is deliberate but always flexible. He's a dream collaborator." —**Ed "Snowdog" Robertson, Lead Singer and Songwriter for Barenaked Ladies**

"*The Greatest Song* is for anyone looking to light up the world with their ideas and artistry. Kevin's rules for creating hit songs, based on his years of hit-making

experience, apply not just to music but to any kind of creative work. They will help you nurture the magical spark you need to bring seemingly crazy ideas to life."
—**Safi Bahcall, Physicist, Biotech Entrepreneur, and *WSJ* Bestselling Author of *Loonshots: How to Nurture the Crazy Ideas That Win Wars, Cure Diseases, and Transform Industries***

"As someone who's experienced the ebb and flow of surviving the music business, I can confidently say Kevin's book follows the perfect path of an artist in an enchanting and inspiring narrative. In addition to his successes in songwriting, producing, and concert festivals, I can't believe that we now have to contend with him as an amazing fiction author too!" —**Mark Volman, The Turtles**

"Never knew how to troubleshoot creativity . . . until now. Kudos to Kevin Griffin."
—**Theo Von, Comedian**

"Kevin Griffin is an integral member of the Nashville music-entertainment scene with his songwriting accolades, the creation of Pilgrimage Music Festival, and now with the release of his book, *The Greatest Song*. His business parable provides tangible insights ideal for anyone looking to boost their own career, woven beautifully through his story surrounding Nashville's iconic songwriting community. Readers will instantly connect with Jake Stark's journey and will walk away feeling empowered to conquer their own day to day. *The Greatest Song* is a compelling read for anyone looking to achieve business success and improved prosperity." —**Dr. Sarita Stewart, Interim Dean of Mike Curb College of Entertainment & Music Business at Belmont University**

"A quick and entertaining read that will provide just the spark you might need for your next innovation. Whether that's a song, a donut flavor, or anything else!"
—**Scott Murphy, President of Dunkin' Donuts**

"*The Greatest Song* is a combination of compelling, fictional story that keeps you turning pages while revealing inspiring advice that you can apply to your career and life. When you feel yourself stuck in your ways, refer to this playbook and get inspired to reach the next level. Bravo, Kevin!" —**Todd Graves, Founder and CEO, Fry Cook, & Cashier, Raising Cane's Chicken Fingers**

"As a professional cowriter (a.k.a. a plus-one), I've spent the bulk of my career collaborative songwriting. After reading my pal, Kevin Griffin's, brilliant *The Greatest Song: Spark Creativity, Ignite Your Career, and Transform Your Life*, I'm starting to rethink all of my previous missteps, and I'm ready to walk on fire! This book is a blueprint for any creative—young or old. It's the absolute truth! I've always resented Kevin for his chiseled looks and effortless studio chops, but now I actually despise him for being a better author as well. I highly recommend you buy his book and sell mine on eBay!" —**Sam Hollander, Songwriter, Producer, and Bestselling Author of *21 Hit Wonder: Flopping My Way to the Top of the Charts***

"This is not just a recipe for the greatest song ever. It is a recipe for a more creative, and ultimately more fulfilling, life. Whether you wish to apply this wisdom to the boardroom or your next big project, there is much wisdom here for anyone who does creative work—which is everyone." —**Jeff Goins, Bestselling Author of** *Real Artists Don't Starve*

"Having written a few songs with Kevin, and after playing many shows with Better Than Ezra, I already had first-hand experience as to his ability to paint a picture with words. This book is a very thoughtful way for Kevin to tell his own story while inspiring us all to maximize our own potential, whether it's professional, creative, or both. Staying relevant in the music business is no small feat. I assume it is like that in most industries. Kevin has it figured out. Great read." —**Jaret Reddick, Singer and Songwriter of Bowling for Soup**

"As a multi-platinum singer/songwriter who's had massive success in this competitive business, Kevin Griffin has experienced what it takes to make it to the top. The advice he shares in these pages will inspire any songwriter hoping to follow him there." —**Mike O'Neill, President and CEO Broadcast Music Inc.**

"Knowing and writing with Kevin Griffin has been one of the highlights of my career. The man is wise and can write a song! Kevin has taken all the knowledge and insight from all his successes and turned it into a great read. *The Greatest Song* should be read by anyone and everyone who is thinking about dipping their toe into this crazy music business." —**Jon McLaughlin, Singer-Songwriter**

"Kevin Griffin writes about the music industry and songwriting from a perspective of established, consistent success. He has every right to offer creative advice, which he does admirably. Written in a story narrative that packs in many songwriting and business details as well as accurate, interesting information about Nashville's Music Row, it is a music industry parable. Intensely interesting, informative, and compelling, this is a great and valuable read." —**Ted Piechocinski, Director of Indiana State University's School of Music and Music Business Program**

"Kevin Griffin is a giver, and this book is a gift. Giving words, lyrics, and choruses to artists and songs comes easy for Kevin, but now in this book, he gives a path through his journey that works and inspires. I am so thankful we collided and collaborated in friendship and business, and I believe that this book will create 'big hits' for those who read it." —**Jeff Sinelli, Founder and Chief Vibe Officer of Which Wich Superior Sandwiches**

"Kevin is such a great guy, and somehow after years in the music industry, he continues to be a great guy! He's always provided me sage-like wisdom and continues to be an inspiration." —**A/J Jackson, Songwriter, Record Producer, and Lead Singer of Saint Motel**

THE GREATEST SONG

THE GREATEST SONG

SPARK *creativity*, IGNITE YOUR CAREER, AND TRANSFORM YOUR LIFE

KEVIN GRIFFIN

BROWN BOOKS
PUBLISHING GROUP

The Greatest Song
Spark Creativity, Ignite Your Career, and Transform Your Life

Brown Books Publishing Group
Dallas, TX/New York, NY
www.BrownBooks.com
(972) 381-0009

A New Era in Publishing®

Publisher's Cataloging-In-Publication Data

Names: Griffin, Kevin, 1968- author.
Title: The greatest song : spark creativity, ignite your career, and transform your life / Kevin Griffin.
Description: Dallas, TX ; New York, NY : Brown Books Publishing Group, [2023]
Identifiers: ISBN: 9781612546032 (paperback) | LCCN: 2022949632
Subjects: LCSH: Music--Vocational guidance. | Popular music--Writing and publishing. | Music trade. | Success. | LCGFT: Creative nonfiction. | BISAC: MUSIC / Business Aspects. | BUSINESS & ECONOMICS / Personal Success.
Classification: LCC: ML3795 .G75 2023 | DDC: 780.23--dc23

ISBN 978-1-61254-603-2
LCCN 2022949632

Printed in the United States
10 9 8 7 6 5 4 3 2 1

For more information or to contact the author, please go to
www.KevinGriffinMusic.com.

For my family

"All children are born artists.
The problem is how to remain an artist as we grow up."
—*Pablo Picasso*

"The more you learn, the more you earn."
—*Warren Buffet*

TABLE OF CONTENTS

INTRODUCTION   1

PROLOGUE   7

CHAPTER 1   The Songwriter   17

CHAPTER 2   The Method   27

CHAPTER 3   Practice One: *Creative Collaboration*   47

CHAPTER 4   Practice Two: *Filling the Well*   63

CHAPTER 5   Great Day   81

CHAPTER 6   Practice Three: *Leaving Your Comfort Zone*   85

CHAPTER 7   Practice Four: *Change Your Attitude*   103

CHAPTER 8   Everybody's Talkin'   119

CHAPTER 9   Practice Five: *Dare to Be Stupid*   129

CHAPTER 10   The Greatest Song   151

CHAPTER 11   Sing It Forward   163

ACKNOWLEDGMENTS   169

ABOUT THE AUTHOR   171

TABLE OF CONTENTS

INTRODUCTION

It's been said before that nothing good happens after 2:00 a.m., and I'm pretty sure that somewhere, at some point, it's also been said that absolutely, *positively* nothing good happens after 2:00 a.m. . . . in a bar . . . in New Orleans . . . during Mardi Gras. I mean, come on, right?

But despite all evidence to the contrary, I would beg to differ. I would even venture to say it is precisely what happened after 2:00 a.m. in a bar—F&M Patio Bar in Uptown New Orleans, to be exact—and during Mardi Gras that is the reason you're reading these words. Something good happened, indeed.

But let me go back a bit.

A few years ago, I was in New Orleans with some friends having been asked to ride on a float in the Hermes parade. Now, if you've ever been to Mardi Gras or seen photos of it, you know that riding on a float is an all-day, all-night affair. And on our way home from the Hermes post-parade masquerade ball, in the wee hours of the morning, some friends and I stopped into F&M's for some late night jambalaya before turning in for some much needed sleep. While I was waiting in line to place my food order, I happened to run into an old friend, Brady Wood. Brady, a businessman and serial entrepreneur, was down in New Orleans with some friends from his YPO (Young Presidents' Organization) group in Dallas. It turned out they had planned a Mardi Gras "educational" trip, and between dinners and parades, they had scheduled a couple of speakers who had been successful in the business world to do presentations for them while in the Big Easy.

As I was asking Brady about the speakers and about what YPO was (a worldwide leadership group of chief executives with almost five hundred different chapters), he casually asked if I'd ever be interested in giving a speech or presentation to his YPO group back in Dallas—maybe talk about the business of music and the songwriting process. Of course, I—being cautious and reserved (ha) and without any prior experience in the speaking world—immediately replied without hesitation, "Yes."

Brady was thrilled, and we agreed to speak on the phone the following week about details. The kitchen called my name, telling me my jambalaya order was ready, and we said our goodbyes.

I really didn't think about Brady or the speech until the next week had rolled around, and before I knew it, it was time for Brady and me to hop on the phone to talk specifics. It was then that I figured it might be a good idea to spend some time thinking about what exactly I would talk about.

Now, I've been in the music business for almost thirty years, starting with my band Better Than Ezra in the '90s, all the way through to founding the Pilgrimage Music and Cultural Festival in Franklin, Tennessee. Along the way, I've had platinum albums, toured the world, and written songs that have been performed and recorded by Taylor Swift, Sugarland, Train, and many others. It's been a crazy, up-and-down-and-up career.

Around about the same time as I ran into Brady down in New Orleans, it so happened that I'd been getting asked more and more by other writers, music magazines, and podcasts about how I had managed to stick around and be successful in a famously fickle industry.

I spent the next couple of hours before the call really thinking about what I've done during my career to stay engaged, inspired, challenged, successful, and ultimately happy. I realized that there were actually things—practices, if you will—that I did on a daily basis to keep an edge and stay in the game of music. What's more, I began to realize that these things weren't specific only to music, but also to any business endeavor or career. I decided that in a speech I could talk about the arc of my career, the ups and downs, and ultimately the things I do—had to do—to continue to evolve in the odd and crazy business of music. Soon, I hopped on the phone with Brady, told him the idea (he loved it), and we locked in a date for the speech in Dallas.

When the YPO event happened a few months later, the speech was met with overwhelming enthusiasm, and the audience (made up of CEOs and leaders of some very well-known companies) asked if I would speak at their respective events. Suddenly, I was doing my speech for companies around the country—and having a blast doing it! At the same time, I realized that the speech was evolving into something different. After each event, people were coming up and telling me that the insights and practices I had shared could help them not just in business, but in life in general.

I started wondering how I could share the speech with more people, not only for companies that had hired me to speak to them, but also for anyone, anywhere, wanting to continue to evolve and grow in their career and in their life . . . someone like *you*. *I'll tell a story,* I thought, while making coffee one morning. That was the "Aha!" moment I'd been waiting on. I sat down at the kitchen table and began the book you're reading now: *The Greatest Song*. And so, without further ado, I give you Jake Stark, journeyman performer and Nashville songwriter. A fictional character, yes, but a very real human with generous parts from my own life thrown in. It's a fun journey of the life of a songwriter banging it out in Nashville—Music City, USA. I hope you get as much out of reading this little story as I have had writing it.

Now, hit PLAY!

SONG *(sòŋ) n.* a short poem or other set of words set to music and meant to be sung or celebrated ‖ consists of five parts: the intro, the verse, the chorus, the bridge, and the coda.

PROLOGUE

Jake Stark, singer-songwriter—*hit* songwriter, that is—stood in front of the imposing wooden doors of Ocean Way Recording Studio, just off Seventeenth Avenue South in the heart of Music Row, Nashville, Tennessee. It had been a long time since Jake had been here . . . too long. This place was legendary in the music world. Housed in a one-hundred-year-old Gothic revival grey stone former church, Ocean Way had seen the likes of George Strait, Garth Brooks, Sheryl Crow, Pink, and even U2 record here. Jake had heard that today—this whole week, in fact—the hot young country band, the Colton Brothers, was recording here.

Well, I guess that's why Chuck asked me to come here, Jake thought, and then felt himself grin as he said out loud, "Folks still want a little of that Jake Stark magic."

Chuck was Chuck Lane, the owner of MegaMusic (Jake's music publisher for the past fifteen or so years), and yesterday Chuck had asked Jake to meet him at the studio to "catch up." Jake figured Chuck wanted to introduce him to the guys in the band so they could set up some songwriting. It was nice timing too. It had been a while since Jake had been asked to be in the room with a recording artist the stature of the Colton Brothers, and it felt good. Not that Jake didn't write with great writers and artists. In a town built on the phrase, "What have you done for me lately?" if you hadn't had a substantial hit in a few years, you weren't gonna get asked to be in a room with an A-level artist. Chuck, though, had always had Jake's back, and it looked like he had delivered again. Jake also couldn't help thinking he could use a boost to his sagging song-writing royalties. They had been going down, and the bills had been piling up.

As Jake pulled open one of the two massive front doors of the studio, a blast of cool air greeted him. He stepped inside. It was still only early spring in Nashville but that didn't mean it wasn't already hot, and the AC felt good. Jake took off his sunglasses, letting his eyes adjust to the softly lit room, and approached the desk of the studio assistant who greeted him with a silent wave.

"Morning. I'm here to see Chuck Lane," Jake said, touching the brim of his Tennessee Titans baseball cap.

"Cool," the assistant, who couldn't have been more than twenty, replied. "May I have your name?"

"Uh . . . Jake Stark," Jake said, remembering a time when everyone in the Nashville music biz knew who he was—even as a kid just starting out.

"Hmmm, I don't see you here on the list." The assistant clicked his tongue as he picked up the receiver of an old-school landline. "Let me just call back . . ."

"It's probably under the Colton Brothers . . ." Jake trailed off as the kid spoke into the receiver.

"Uh-huh, okay. I'll send him back." The assistant looked up at Jake as he hung up the phone and pointed to a door behind hm. "Mr. Lane is just off Studio A in the green room. Through the door and down the hallway."

"Yep, know it well. Thanks." Jake nodded his head as he walked past the desk and opened the door to the hallway that led to the studios.

One of Jake's favorite things about Ocean Way was this hallway. On the walls, covering every available square inch of space, were platinum and gold records from just about every artist you could imagine. It was stunning, really, the level of musicianship and talent that had passed down this hallway and worked in these three studios. And now Jake was here again, going to the main studio, Studio A . . . or at least the kitchen of Studio A.

Toward the end of the hallway, on his left, the platinum- and gold-album-lined wall gave way to a long window looking into the interior of the vast church that now served as the main tracking room of A. Jake had never met the members of the Colton Brothers, but he knew what they looked like. And right now, they were all playing. The drummer, guitarists, and bass player all faced each other in a large circle in the center of the studio.

Wow, already tracking at 10:30 a.m. . . . back in the day that's about when I'd be waking up, Jake thought as he reached the end of the hallway and went through the door on the right marked "Green Room."

Studio A's green room was suitably plush: dimly lit with tastefully modern furniture, a full wet bar, and what must have been an eighty-inch flatscreen at the far end of the room. There, standing with his back to Jake, framed by the muted TV tuned to ESPN *Sportscenter*, was Chuck Lane, veteran Nashville music publisher.

"Well, there he is. The myth, the legend . . ." Jake spoke as he walked in the room. "Chuck Lane, folks!"

Chuck Lane, sixty-ish and trim with a darker-than-it-should-have-been-at-his-age full head of brown hair, wheeled around on the heels of his ostrich-skin cowboy boots.

"My man, how are you?" Chuck held his hands out as he walked toward Jake. "Looking good as ever. How do you do it?"

"Ha ha, well that's mighty nice of you to say. I'm great."

They gave each other a hug—a Nashville hug, they called it. It's the first thing you notice when you move to the Music City; everybody in the music business hugs: a quick, noncommittal, upper-body-only-touching hug. "It has been way too long." Chuck stepped back toward the TV. "When was the last time we saw each other in person?"

"*CMA Awards* two years ago . . ." Jake said and then thought, *And I've tried to get appointments to see you, but that ain't happening if I don't have at least a current Top Ten song.* Jake hadn't had a charting song in . . . a long time.

"Well, crap, that's way too long."

"Hey man, no worries. We're here now, and with the Colton Brothers to boot." Jake motioned behind him toward the Studio A tracking room. "They are on fire right now."

Chuck looked a little confused and then raised his eyebrows.

"Oh, that's right, they're here in Studio A. I saw that. Yeah, they're hitting on all cylinders for sure."

"How long you been working with them?" Jake asked as he put his sunglasses on the little dining table.

"Oh . . . No, I wish. Tried to sign them a few years ago, but they ended up going to Sony Publishing after a bit of a bidding war. Got too rich for my blood," Chuck said as he walked over to the wet bar.

"Gotcha. Well, why are you here at Ocean Way?" Jake caught a Lacroix water from Chuck who was rummaging through the refrigerator. "Yeah, I got a baby band with some writers I signed in Studio C," Chuck said, still looking around in the refrigerator. "They're letting us share this green room while they remodel C's."

Jake opened the water as the sting of recognition took hold. Chuck hadn't asked him here to write with the Colton Brothers. He was here to work with some baby band just starting out. Still though, work was work.

"Gotcha," Jake said, taking a sip. "What's the story with—"
"Listen, Jake," Chuck interrupted. "Oh, sorry. Go ahead."

"All good," Jake replied. "I was just asking the name of the band."

"My band? Oh, in Studio C." Chuck closed the refrigerator door. "They're a little bluegrass band called The Adirondacks."

"Oh, cool." Jake took another sip of the Lacroix as his hopes for a good write dipped even further. He liked bluegrass, but bluegrass wasn't going to be played on the radio. Translation: this wasn't going to be a write that would re-launch his career or make any money. And money was needed.

"But hey, I wanted to speak with you face-to-face," Chuck said, and Jake could sense that he was a bit uncomfortable. "As you know, your publishing deal is almost up."

"End of this month, in fact." Jake looked at his watch. "About time to re-up!"

"Yeah, it's about up, for sure . . ." Chuck paused, then continued, "but, you know, that's why I wanted to talk to you this morning."

"I'm all yours."

"Good, good. So we've been together now like . . . what's it been, ten years?" Chuck asked.

"Actually, it's been closer to fifteen years," Jake replied, and did not like the feeling he was beginning to get.

"Wow, that's right. Julie had just been born when we signed you. I left the hospital for the signing party." Julie was Chuck's daughter. He continued, "Damn, time flies . . ."

"Oh yeah, it does." Jake took a sip of his water. "Especially when you've had as many hits as we've had together."

"Great times, and yes, hits galore in the day." Chuck was fidgeting as he talked, something Jake hadn't seen him do before. "But, you know, we're at kind of a bit of a crossroads."

"How do you mean?"

"Well, Jake, I'm just going to be straight with you." Chuck stopped his fidgeting and looked Jake in the eyes. "We're not . . . we can't, uh, pick up your option for your publishing deal."

"Wait, what?" Jake was blindsided.

"Jake, the advance for your option is large, too large, given that—"

"Given that what?" Jake said, cutting off Chuck but tempering his emotions.

"Well, given that it's been five or six years since you had any, you know, action. Well, big action, anyway, with your songwriting," Chuck replied, and Jake could see Chuck didn't like the conversation any more than he did, but Jake couldn't help being annoyed.

"Chuck, the royalties I have coming into you guys are still substantial. It doesn't make sense that you guys would want to move on."

"Yes, they are substantial, but those are recurring royalties for your catalog, the old hits that, honestly, we'll have whether we re-sign you or not," Chuck said and kept talking. "Look, you know, you know that no one is a bigger fan of Jake Stark than me."

"It doesn't really feel that way right now." Jake tried to chuckle, but couldn't manage even a smile.

"I just think . . . and I've been here before with a few of my big writers over the course of my career," Chuck said. "I just think that you might benefit from a new team. You know, that has fresh ideas and new people for you to work with."

"Mm-hmm," Jake murmured.

"I mean, we've just been doing things the same way with you, the same writers, the same everything, and it's just not working the way you or I want it to." Chuck put his hands up in supplication. "And full disclosure, I am an independent publisher, as you know, and I could use the money that I would spend on re-upping you to sign four-to-five new songwriters."

"Unproven, no-hits-yet songwriters," Jake said as he raised an eyebrow and nodded his head slowly. "Look, you're right about not being where I want to be career-wise, but I hadn't considered leaving MegaMusic. And now, you're showing me the door."

"No, no I'm not, Jake," Chuck said and mustered a smile. "I really, *really* do think that this will be the best thing for both of us, but especially you. Look, I'm not blowing smoke. I think you have a lot more ahead of you. I just don't know how to get you there. And what's that they say? Nothing changes if nothing changes."

"Well," Jake said as he put the Lacroix down on the table, "for what it's worth, I do think I have a lot ahead of me, my best work, but now I gotta go out and scrounge around for a new publisher." Jake looked down at his watch. "And look at that, I have a write in thirty at my studio, so I guess I better hustle."

"Brother, you have tons in front of you." Chuck put his hand on Jake's shoulder, "I'm probably gonna regret this."

"Oh yeah, you sure as hell will," Jake said as he looked Chuck in the eye, smiled, and shook his hand. He wasn't going to leave the room defeated, but defeated is exactly how he felt as he turned to open up the door to the long, platinum-lined hallway. "I'm sure I'll bump into you soon."

"You will, Jake. Take care, buddy." And with that, Jake Stark was suddenly a writer without a publishing deal in Nashville—the last thing you want to be. Right back where he was twenty-five years ago, but this time he wasn't twenty years old; he was forty-five. As he walked down the hall toward the reception room, he couldn't help but feel that, in some way, he was leaving behind success and everything he'd been used to. The word that no one in Nashville—or anywhere else, for that matter—ever wants uttered around their name floated in his head.

Has-been.

Well, that just happened, Jake thought as he pushed open the reception door. The kid at the desk turned in his chair.

"Wow, that was fast. Have a good one."

"Uh-huh, will do." Jake couldn't help but roll his eyes ever so slightly. He couldn't get out of there fast enough, and walked across the room in four long strides. Getting to the two large front doors of Ocean Way, he pushed them both open and stepped out into the rising heat.

Damn, my sunglasses. Left 'em in the green room, Jake thought, as he squinted up at the sun. *Ugh, just go back and get 'em, Jake. You can do this. Painless.*

He turned around before the doors closed and slid back inside.

"Be quick. Left my sunglasses in the green room," Jake said, shrugging to the assistant. And though it wasn't the case, inside Jake felt like suddenly the kid looked at him differently, like he knew Chuck had just let him go. It was the look you gave to a . . . a has-been.

C'mon, Jake, don't be silly, Jake said to himself as he moved swiftly back down the platinum-lined hallway to the green room door.

When he stepped into the room, Chuck was gone, but another guy was there, bending over, looking into the refrigerator. At the sound of the green room door opening, he popped his head up and looked directly at Jake who instantly recognized him as Garrett Colton, the singer of the Colton Brothers. Jake couldn't help but know who he was. Colton had been dating some of the biggest female artists in country and pop the past couple of years. He was everywhere on social media and gossip rags.

"Well, hey man, good to see you," Garrett said with a bright look on his face.

Ah, he recognizes me, Jake thought and, at this moment, after the conversation with Chuck, it felt good.

"Hey, good to see you, as well. Just grabbing my sunglasses and I'll be out of your hair," Jake said with an exaggerated reach for the glasses. *Well, I might not be writing with him, but at least he knows who I am. I got that at least.*

"You're just the guy I've been looking for," Garrett said as he looked back in the fridge.

"Well, alright," Jake said hopefully in his best cowboy voice as he grabbed his glasses and paused. *Was the day about to be salvaged with a write after all? What did Chuck know . . .?*

"Yeah, man," Garrett Colton put his head back into the fridge, "any way you could stock this fridge with some more sodas? Cokes and stuff? We're all out."

"Uh . . ." A rush of crushing embarrassment hit him like a truck. Garrett Colton didn't recognize him, no, not at all. He thought Jake was an assistant at the studio, someone who stocked the green room. Jake was momentarily speechless.

"You got 'em around?" Garrett asked with his head still in the refrigerator.

"Yeah, yeah . . ." Jake somehow found words. "Let me, uh, go check. Be right back."

Jake quickly exited the room as he heard Colton say from behind, "Thanks, partner."

There was a ringing in Jake's ears, and his face felt flushed. The gold and platinum albums on the hallway wall blurred past as he quickly reached the door to the reception room.

"Well, you're still here? Ha, have a good one," said the receptionist as Jake moved quickly through the room to the exit doors which, at the moment, seemed impossibly far to Jake. He felt dizzy. He didn't answer the kid. A text chimed on his cell. It was from Sarah, Jake's wife.

How's it going?! 👍

He put the phone in his pocket.

Just get me out of here! Jake's thoughts were practically screaming.

A potent blend of ego, fear, annoyance, and severe embarrassment filled Jake, almost swallowing him. This was the exact opposite of what he had thought the day would bring.

What am I gonna do now? Jake thought as he pushed the doors open into the rising heat of a Nashville spring day. *No publishing deal, no current hits, and plenty of bills. Great.*

And, unlike when Jake had arrived just twenty minutes earlier, the sun didn't look bright and hopeful. It was blinding.

Chapter 1

THE SONGWRITER

Jake Stark's week couldn't get much worse. He hadn't imagined it. MegaMusic Publishers really wasn't renewing his contract. He could hear Chuck Lane's voice: matter-of-fact, strictly business, as if he were trading in a used car. At least, that's how it felt to Jake right now. He'd always been a realist about his career, told himself he wasn't the type to get his feelings hurt, but this had come out of left field at a moment he'd least expected it.

Now, this is *the* Jake Stark. Hit songwriter Jake Stark, who'd had a respectable career as a recording artist in the early 1990s. The Jake Stark who was twenty-one years old when he was signed to his first record deal, who had a debut album that went platinum and another that went gold. The same guy who had toured the world opening for REM, Tears for Fears, Oasis, and Lionel Richie when he wasn't headlining clubs and theaters around the country. The Jake Stark who'd been number forty-one on *People's* "50 Most Beautiful People" list in 1993. The same Jake Stark who, as his own recording career began to falter, started writing hits for Garth Brooks, The Chicks, and Madonna. That's right, the Jake Stark who had written hits—*number one* hits—for country artists as well as pop artists, a rare feat at any time, but especially in the '90s. That string of hits had continued up until the early 2000s.

And then, well . . . the hits just quit coming, or at least they'd quit coming as fast. Since, oh, 2004, Jake just hadn't had the massive hits that he had become known for. In fact, in the past five or so years—okay, fine, in the past *ten* years—Jake hadn't had a number one song. He'd started as the hottest writer in Nashville, always the youngest guy in the studio. Now at forty-five, he wasn't broke, but *pretty* damn close, and feeling like just another washed-up Nashville writer without a publishing deal. Visions of selling cars or getting his real estate license floated in his head. How did he end up here?

Jake parked his '98 Range Rover on Edgehill Drive, just off Music Row. Looking in the rearview mirror, he ran his hand over three days of graying stubble.

It's not the '90s anymore, pal, Jake thought to himself, *but you still got a little left in the tank.*

He got out of the vehicle and crossed the street to Taco Amigo to meet with Brice Smith, who had messaged him yesterday out of the blue. Friday at Taco Amigos was a total scene. Players and wannabe players starting the weekend early with two-for-one margaritas. He knew this place would be a madhouse today, but Brice liked noise as much as he liked crowds.

Centered on Sixteenth and Seventeenth Avenues South, Music Row was nestled in Nashville's historic district. The history ran long and deep on these blocks, and if you worked in the music biz in Nashville, anywhere from record labels to radio stations, chances were you worked in a building somewhere nearby. Back in the day, Elvis, Frank Sinatra, and the Beatles had recorded here at the famed RCA Studios. Now, you might find Harry Styles, Keith Urban, or Adele in a studio around here.

It had once been just old homes, craftsman houses from the 1950s that housed all manner of music businesses; but in the past twenty years—and especially recently—big businesses had moved in with modern buildings, parking garages, and such. Banks, venture capital firms, and boutique hotels stood shoulder to shoulder with the old Music Row architecture, but the transition was bigger than that. Nashville was in a constant battle between its country music roots and the new reality that the city was a world center of the music industry, not just the home of country. Jake could literally see that shift walking through Music Row.

Once in Taco Amigo, Jake was struck by the clash of different people. Old-school Nashville, all Wranglers and cowboy boots, mixed effortlessly with new Nashville in skinny jeans and designer sneakers. Standing at the hostess station, Jake took it in until he caught sight of Brice waving to him from a booth in the back. As Jake navigated the packed restaurant, he remembered that Brice Smith had been in Nashville almost as long as he had. He'd had good cuts along the way. Nothing like Jake's success, but still, a respectable career. In the past couple of years though, Brice had been on fire. He'd had a string of number ones and was one of the most sought-after songwriters anywhere. He'd also signed a deal with a small boutique publishing company, The Row, which—for a couple of years—had been the talk of both Nashville and the local gossip mill. It was the pet project of Daniel Smith-Daniels, a British billionaire who'd made a fortune developing some kind of groundbreaking financial software.

Turns out Daniel had been a child prodigy in mathematics *and* music. At fifteen he'd been offered scholarships to MIT, Harvard, Oxford, Julliard . . . the list went on. But instead, he chose to attend the London Business School, and when he wasn't in classes or workshops, he could be found busking on streets or sitting in with different bands in local pubs. As a student at LBS, Smith-Daniels began developing a revolutionary algorithm with specific applications in the financial world. By using "predictive analytics," a form of AI, he could determine—with *stunning* accuracy—trends in the stock market and the London Metal Exchange. It was concrete data that would make the user of this algorithm very rich. As word got out about Smith-Daniels and his groundbreaking work, job offers began piling up. By seventeen, he had graduated from LBS, and rather than accept a lucrative job from any one of a dozen top financial firms and technology companies, he founded his own company, Muse Analytics, with seed money from a small pool of investors.

In short order, the company exploded. Smith-Daniels's software was licensed throughout the world, and fortunes were made, including one for him. At twenty-two, he cashed out, selling a majority stake in Muse Analytics for north of $5 billion. He next devoted himself to philanthropy and—you guessed it—music. At twenty-four, he became the youngest person in modern times to be knighted, mainly for his work in tackling the persistent poverty in the developing world. Yeah, knighted, as in get down on one knee and the Queen of England takes a sword and . . . well, you get the picture.

By applying the same algorithm he'd used in the financial world to supply chain problems endemic to developing countries, Smith-Daniels's program was having real, tangible effects in diminishing poverty and raising standards of living throughout Africa. As if being knighted weren't enough, he broke ground on The Row—his newly founded music publishing company in Nashville—that same year. He'd also unveiled TuneCocoon, once again applying his financial world algorithm to the music industry. It quickly became the industry standard for record and streaming companies. In reality, it was a series of warehouses, what he called "memory farms," south of town near Franklin.

The British press had dubbed him Sir Kid—not the kind of thing that would win you any favors in Nashville. He fancied himself a songwriter, a "musician at heart" (cue the collective groan), hence the leap into the music industry. But other than the gossip, most of Nashville had turned a blind eye to The Row, at least until the hit songs, written by a small stable of writers, began to speak for themselves.

Still though, how'd Brice go from middle-of-the-road songwriter to hitmaker?

Give me some of that, thought Jake as he sat down in the booth across from Brice. *What's the secret sauce?*

"Jake Stark, ladies and gentlemen." Brice touched the brim of his baseball cap with a tortilla chip. "I salute you! What's going on, pal?"

Brice had always been a guy with a bright personality, always in a good mood, but right now he seemed to glow. *Man, success has an effect on people,* Jake thought.

"Ha! Brice, good to see you, my brother." Jake settled in the booth. "I'm good, but it's been a helluva week."

"Well, I'd be lying if I said I hadn't heard." Brice scooped up a chunk of guacamole. "Word travels quick around Nashville, as you know . . . smoke signals and such."

"Yeah, it was a good run with Chuck and the boys and girls at MegaMusic, but everything runs its course." Jake grabbed a chip. "I think it was just time to move on."

"I hear you," Brice said. "Change is good. Actually, it's essential. I'm living proof, man."

They spent the next fifteen minutes catching up with each other—family, business, funny stories from their past, and industry gossip. There was always some juicy story about a label head or some temperamental artist getting fired or dropped from their label, or an uplifting story about a great young artist getting signed to a record deal. Of course, the best stories were the ones with scandal— somebody getting what was coming to them. Nashville might be a few thousand miles from Germany, but it was no stranger to *schadenfreude.* When their lunch came, the conversation turned back to Jake's week.

"So, what do you think is next, Jake?" Brice took a bite of his food. "Where's your head at?"

"You know what?" Jake leaned forward. "Honestly? I want to be back on top. I want to be back where I was . . . jeesh, ten years ago when it was crazy. I mean, I still think I have that career-defining song in me. I still want to write the greatest song ever." He let out a little laugh.

Brice raised his eyebrows and leaned forward a bit. "You're serious, aren't you?"

He nodded. "I've been going through some old emails and calendars while getting my catalog together, and it was nuts how much I had going on. And when I think about it, I really don't know why it stopped, or at least trailed off, you know? I mean, it's not like I started doing anything differently."

"Ah," Brice held his finger up, and a smile appeared on his face. "Maybe that's your problem."

"Huh?" Jake leaned back in the booth.

"Not doing anything differently," Brice said. "Maybe that's the reason you're not where you want to be career-wise."

"Dude, let's be honest. We're talking life-wise." Jake shook his head. "My life is a mess in general."

"Perfect," Brice exclaimed. That wasn't the response Jake expected, but Brice went on. "So you think you're ready to mix it up? Try a different approach?"

"Brother, at this point, I'm up for anything." Jake forced a smile but felt cautious. "But you're not about to get weird on me, are you? What you got up your sleeve?"

Brice laughed loudly. "Right? No, man, I just want to know where your head's at, and honestly, you sound like me a couple years ago."

"God help me, I'm screwed," Jake said with a deep laugh and more than a little emotion.

"Seriously, though," Brice continued, "I was in the same place you are, but worse. I never had the success you had. It was bad. I was having trouble paying bills. I was thinking about hanging it up, taking the family back home to Massachusetts. But then, it turned around."

"Wait, let me guess." Jake grabbed a tortilla chip and put the tip to his temple, mind-reader style. He closed his eyes. "Uh . . . Sir Kid? Sir Kid turned it all around?"

Brice smiled and put up his hands, "Ha, you're good, but in a word, *yes*. It started with meeting Daniel, or as you called him, Sir Kid, but ultimately, it wasn't him so much as it was his *method* or as he would say . . . *The* Method."

"The method for what, songwriting?" Jake couldn't keep the skepticism from his voice.

"Yeah, for songwriting, but it's bigger than that. It's more like a method for life, really. That's actually kind of the reason I DMed you yesterday. Daniel, uh, Sir Kid and I were talking about you."

"Wait, what?" Jake didn't expect anyone to be talking about him anymore, unless it was a where-are-they-now conversation, and he certainly didn't expect a British billionaire to be talking about him. As dubious as Jake was about anything called "The Method," he had to admit, his interest was piqued.

"Yep, earlier this week he brought your name up. He wants to meet you."

"You know, if I didn't know better, I'd say you were messing with me. A billionaire known as Sir Kid, twenty-eight years old—"

"Twenty-seven," Brice corrected him.

"Yeah, exactly! A twenty-seven-year-old billionaire wants to meet me, Jake Stark, washed-up artist and struggling songwriter?"

"Precisely," Brice grinned. "Whatcha say? Wanna turn it around? Wanna turn it all around?"

Jake paused. His instinct was to say something smart, but for once, he thought better of it.

"You know . . . What have I got to lose? Ain't like I've got anything better to do. Why not? I'll meet Sir Kid." It sounded strange, silly even, saying it.

"Perfect," Brice told him. "I'll shoot you his number."

"Okay, so what do I tell his assistant when I call?" Jake slid out of the booth as he began to follow Brice out of the restaurant. They snaked out quickly, and Brice turned to Jake once they were outside.

"No, I'm not giving you his assistant's number. I'm giving you his. Daniel's. He wants to talk to you."

"As if this week couldn't get any stranger, Brice. One minute I'm getting dropped from my longtime publisher and the next, I'm getting a billionaire's number to call so we can shoot the breeze."

"You'll see that it's really not that strange after all. And you're gonna do more than shoot the breeze with Daniel. If you really want to turn things around, you're going to get to work. The Method is work." Brice shook Jake's hand and slapped his shoulder. "I'll shoot you the number from my car. Oh, and can't wait to hear it!"

He started to walk away and then called back. "Uh, hear what?"

"The greatest song ever, of course."

"Oh, ha, yeah. Will send it right over to you," Jake called back as he walked down the Taco Amigo steps to Edgehill Drive. His head was spinning.

What just happened? An hour ago, he'd felt at a loss, desperate, but now, now he was walking on air, giddy even. *The billionaire, Sir Kid, wants to see yours truly . . . Well, of course he does. Don't call it a comeback!*

Jake was almost strutting down the sidewalk when he got to his Rover . . . or where it should have been. The spot was empty, and when he looked up the street, there was his beat-up Rover being towed away.

"No! Damnit!" Jake smacked his hands together as the tow truck turned down Sixteenth Street. Jake looked at the street sign that said, of course: NO PARKING. TOW-AWAY ZONE.

Well, crap, Jake thought. *Looks like I'm gonna be walking to the tow truck yard.*

You don't deserve an Uber, Jake.

"Don't call it a comeback," Jake said out loud as he began following the tow truck on foot. "Call it a walk-back."

Just then his phone buzzed with a message from Brice.

> Daniel Smith-Daniels
> 615-654-7654.
> Call him tomorrow at 8:30 a.m.

Jake responded with a thumbs-up emoji. *8:30 a.m.?* he thought. *Damn, that was early, and on a Saturday.*

Oh, and give my best to Sarah and Mac!

Will do!

As Jake answered, he thought about his wife and twelve-year-old son. Jake couldn't quite put his finger on it, but over the past few months—hell, over the past few years—he'd just felt more and more disconnected from them, and it gnawed at him. After a bad relationship with a good woman, he had been careful about committing to Sarah until he was sure she understood the often crazy rules of his business. They'd never had any problems, and even now, all he felt was something akin to . . . what? Distance? Maybe it was his stalled career or something else, but whatever it was, Jake knew he needed to fix it.

In the warm air of an early springtime evening in Nashville, a light drizzle began to fall on Music Row, and Jake Stark, songwriter, just had to smile and laugh. As he walked toward Music Row Towers, the words to one of his favorite songs popped into his head—an old B. J. Thomas classic written by Burt Bacharach for the movie *Butch Cassidy and the Sundance Kid*. Jake began to sing out loud.

"Rain drops keep falling on my head . . ."

Chapter 2

THE METHOD

The next morning at 7:30 a.m. sharp, Jake's alarm went off with the same song he'd used to wake up to for the better part of ten years, "Everybody's Talkin'," by the late, great Harry Nilsson. Jake lay in bed for a couple minutes, soaking up the classic song and its hypnotic finger-picked guitar part.

They don't write 'em like they used to, thought Jake, half awake. *Now it's just a bunch of prefab crap on the radio.*

Sarah, ever the early riser, was already up and had probably finished a run by now.

Jake lay there a bit longer. Just as he was about to drag himself from the bed and go make a coffee before calling Smith-Daniels, his phone rang. Jake picked it up off the bedside table and looked at the screen. "SIR KID" stood out in stark relief on the iPhone touch screen. That's how he'd labeled Daniel Smith-Daniels's number in his phone contacts last night.

Jake quickly cleared his throat and sat up in bed. He did a quick pat on each cheek to wake up and then he hit the green button.

"Hello?" Jake's voice came out a little croakier than he would have liked.

"Good morning, Jake," a young sounding voice with a clipped British accent greeted him. "Daniel Smith-Daniels here. How are you?"

"Great, hello . . . Nice to meet you." Jake was still waking up.

"The pleasure is mine. Forgive the early call. I flew in from London yesterday, and my body is still on Greenwich Mean Time.

I've been up since 4:00 a.m." Daniel sounded a little too chipper for Jake's waking ears.

"Ha, well, that's about the time I went to bed." Jake then realized that might not be the best thing to say to a prospective new publisher, a billionaire wunderkind interested in spending time with Jake Stark.

"Jake, I know we had planned to just speak on the phone this morning." He could already tell this guy was the real deal by the confidence and poise in his voice. "But perhaps you can just come by The Row at our original time, and we can chat face-to-face. We could have breakfast, as well. Would that work?"

"Well sure, Daniel," Jake looked at the clock. 7:45 a.m. "That's no problem. I live ten minutes away in Green Hills. I'll be there!"

"Brilliant, Jake. Until then."

"Sounds good. Bye."

"Cheers." The line went dead.

Well, okay, Jake thought as he dragged himself out of bed and to the shower. *Here we go. This is gonna be interesting.*

Once Jake had retrieved his towed Rover and returned to his Green Hills home last night, he'd gone online and dug deeper into just how Smith-Daniels had made his fortune and found his way to Nashville, of all places.

In the shower, Jake went over Smith-Daniels's story in his mind. From the daunting task of monetizing ever-changing digital distribution challenges to predicting hit songs, TuneCocoon was the be-all and end-all. Despite all that, for the past couple of years, Smith-Daniels had devoted most of his time to music: writing music and building The Row. In an article Jake had read, Smith-Daniels said he was interested in how the mathematics of music defied quantification. Yes, it could be rigid and adhered to certain "musical math," but the subjective nature of music was an elusive thing. That was what compelled him to spend so much time on it. The fact that music, more than anything, existed between the lines of rigid thought and dogma, that it refused to be cornered by anything approaching the scientific method—*that* was what obsessed and inspired Daniel Smith-Daniels.

I never realized I was such a scientific anomaly, Jake thought as he got out of the shower, *just picking up a guitar and singing a song.*

In twenty-five minutes, Jake was in the old Rover as it chugged along Hillsboro Drive on the way to Music Row. At a red light, he checked his phone for emails.

"Ugh," Jake said out loud as he saw another email from Cal Turner, a distant high school friend, someone he hadn't seen or spoken to in years, until, well, until Jake's mother had given his email to Cal after he'd reached out to her on Facebook. *Gotta speak to Mom about that,* he thought.

Anyhow, Cal had been emailing incessantly about Jake getting together and writing a song with his daughter, a budding singer/songwriter studying music business at Belmont College, a small university with a world-class music program situated just off Music Row. This kind of request came all the time for guys like Jake. The son or daughter of an old friend is dreaming of "making it" in the music business, so they call the one friend in their life connected to the biz. Jake scanned the email and saw that now Cal had attached an MP3 of one of his daughter's songs: "Over It."

"Over it" is right, he thought, as the light turned green, and he shut off the phone screen.

Soon Jake was rolling down Seventeenth Avenue South past the brand-new Virgin Hotel, past the Sony Building, past all the staggering musical history that was Music City, and then, there it was—The Row. Beautiful. Stunning really, but it stuck out like a sore thumb sandwiched between a drab 1980s-era office building on one side and a quaint craftsman cottage on the other.

Jeesh, Jake thought, slowing down in front of the building. Six gleaming, twisting, and undulating stories of burnished metal and glass shimmered in the early morning sun. The building was breathtaking, framed against the clear, cobalt-blue Nashville sky. It was like something the great architect, Frank Gehry, would have designed . . . had Frank Gehry ever shotgunned three Red Bulls and got to drawing. Toward the far end of the building was the entrance to the parking garage, or at least, that's what he assumed. There was a turn cut into the curb, but it appeared that there was no entrance. The drive just dead-ended into the building. Jake turned off Seventeenth anyway, and he then noticed a sleek, almost invisible pylon that rose from the concrete.

"Ah," he said, and turned down the radio. He inched the Rover up and lowered the window. There was a single camera lens and speaker on the pylon. No keypad or anything else. As soon as the window was down, a soft and pleasant tone, like a mallet on a meditation bowl, emanated from the speaker, and then a voice.

"Jake. Brilliant, you're here." Daniel Smith-Daniels's ever-chipper voice came forth from the speaker. "Pull forward, and the wall will open. I'll meet you in the foyer."

"All good, man. See you in a sec." Jake said as he raised the window. *Damn,* he thought, *pretty impressive. A billionaire waiting to greet little old Jake Stark . . . and he answered the parking gate!*

Jake eased the Rover forward, and the undulating wall opened silently from the center and receded to the left and right as Jake pulled into the parking structure. A lone gleaming black Tesla Model S was parked ahead of him, and Jake pulled the old Rover into the space next to the stunning vehicle.

"Hey, listen, don't be intimidated, girl," Jake said as he patted the Rover's dashboard. He eyed the Model S as he cut the engine. *But I wouldn't mind getting my hands on one of those.*

Jake hopped out of the Rover and reached back into the vehicle to grab his satchel—his "man purse," as his friends called it. The wall of the parking garage closed again. Silently. As in no sound. As in a crazy-expensive-to-engineer mechanism. As in *I want one of those for myself,* Jake thought. Coming out from between the cars, Jake turned to his left toward two glass doors. As he approached, the doors opened into a warmly lit area with modern, minimalist furniture. There, standing in the center of the room, was Daniel Smith-Daniels.

Now Jake wasn't into fashion exactly, but he still knew good and expensive taste when he saw it. Smith-Daniels wore perfectly fitted Chinos, a black T-shirt (James Perse, if Jake had to guess), and a lightweight Moncler down vest.

"Well, there he is. The legend, Jake Stark!" Daniel walked toward Jake and extended his hand. "Welcome to The Row."

"Why, thanks. Pleasure to meet you, man!" Jake shook Daniel's hand.

"The pleasure is mine, really," Smith-Daniels said. "And thanks again for coming so early on a Saturday morning. Shall we have breakfast?"

"Brother, I am famished." Jake followed Daniel into an open elevator against the far wall. "Haven't had anything since . . . Well, dinner last night with our mutual friend, Brice."

"Ah, Brice," Smith-Daniels replied as he pushed the button. "He is on quite a roll right now. Couldn't be happening to a more deserving fellow, I might add." Jake noted that The Row's six stories were numbered in the European fashion. The first story was the ground floor, then there was the first floor above that, and so on. They were going to the top floor of the six-story building . . . the fifth floor.

"Yeah, Brice and I go back quite a ways. We've both been kicking around these parts for a while." Jake felt the elevator moving smoothly upward. "Good to see him finding success."

"Ah well, there's the rub." Smith-Daniels turned from facing the closed doors of the elevator to look directly at Jake. "Finding success . . . well, that's the easy part, isn't it?" He smiled at Jake.

"Well . . ." Jake wasn't sure where this guy was heading.

"Yes, finding success. We do that all the time to a greater or lesser degree, don't we?" Daniel raised an eyebrow, Spock-like, to Jake. A beat passed. "Now *keeping* success, that's the hard part. *That's* the elusive quarry. That's what Brice is doing. He's *keeping* and growing success. That's what we do at The Row."

Just then, the elevator doors opened, and a woman dressed in smart black jeans, gray suede Chelsea boots, and a vintage Rolling Stones T-shirt stood smiling at Daniel.

"Misha, good morning." Daniel stepped from the elevator along with Jake. "So good of you to come in on a Saturday. Thank you. Meet the talented Jake Stark."

"Good morning." Jake extended his hand. "Pleasure to meet you, Misha."

"Nice to meet you, as well," Misha smiled, nodded at Jake, and then looked back at Daniel. "Good timing, boys. Breakfast is served in the garden."

"Ah, excellent. I'm quite peckish." Daniel smiled and patted his stomach.

The three of them moved into yet another impressive room. Ahead and to the left was a sitting area made up of sleek, modern Italian furniture tastefully arranged on bleached herringbone-patterned wood floors. Several huge Francesco Clemente prints looked down from the walls. To the right was a classic Eames reception desk.

"Jake, Misha is enjoying her first number-one song right now. Thomas Rhett's 'C'mon, Girl.' She's also an *amazing* chef. Oh, and if that weren't enough, she has a doctorate in psychology, as well."

"Wow, is that all?" Jake deadpanned. He got the laughs he was looking for from Daniel and Misha.

"Ah, Daniel flatters me, Jake." Misha walked toward a door next to the reception desk. "Really, though, I was a professional student for far too long. My parents must have detested it. I was too happy traveling the world and living out of a backpack."

"That doesn't sound so bad," Jake said.

"The greatest time ever, Jake," Misha said, a little wistfully. "At any rate, your breakfast is going to be cold if you two don't get to it."

Daniel gestured for Jake to follow after Misha and, as Jake walked through the open door, he was blown away by the expanse and beauty of the office . . . if you could call it that. It seemed to be much more. Taking up what must have been the majority of the fifth floor, this great open room instantly felt like a creative playland. It was amazing.

Jake immediately noticed the white terrazzo floors inlaid with beautifully intricate designs—like looking through a kaleidoscope, only they were walking on it. In the center of the room, sitting on overlaid *kilim* rugs, was a grouping of furniture around a recording desk with a computer, recording gear, mics, guitars, and a gorgeous old upright piano. In one corner were vintage pinball machines and a ping-pong table. In the opposite corner was a wet bar, and scattered throughout the room were skateboards, a mountain bike, and one of those single-wheel electric hover boards. It was a thoroughly cool and modern recording room and creative space, like something out of a movie. Jake followed Misha as she walked to the far end of the room, where a retractable wall opened to the sunlight and greenery beyond.

"Daniel," Jake looked around as he spoke, "this room is badass." That was the only way he could think to describe it.

"Thank you, Jake. I think so too." Smith-Daniels followed behind him. "It must be open and fun, and . . . precisely badass."

Jake reached the far end of the room and stepped outside. It was like going through a time warp, as if he had been transported. They had been in an expansive, modern writing room/office in Nashville, but suddenly they had stepped into an English garden smack-dab in the middle of Music Row.

Manicured boxwoods lined a pea gravel path that went through a bougainvillea-covered archway. Sculpted topiaries were strategically placed throughout the rooftop garden, and lavender, marigolds, and foxglove bloomed. Birds chirped, and Jake saw a hummingbird at a feeder.

Turning right after the archway, they came upon a wrought iron and glass table where a delicious-looking breakfast awaited them.

"This is amazing, you guys. Breathtaking." Jake was blown away. "I've passed this building for a couple years now, and I had no idea this was here." He walked to the vine-covered railing of the garden and looked down on Seventeenth Avenue South. Yep, there it was. He was still in Nashville after all.

"It's our secret garden. I decided this place needed a little something from England—a respite from Nashville." Daniel gestured to the table. "Shall we eat?"

"Yes, please." Jake walked over to the table, the gravel crunching under his feet.

"Right then," said Misha, walking back to the archway. "Jake, if I don't see you again today, it was a pleasure. Enjoy your meeting."

In front of Jake was a mouthwatering spread with fruit, poached eggs, smoked salmon, a breadbasket—the whole works. He dug in, and Daniel followed suit. After a moment, Jake spoke.

"Well, this doesn't suck," Jake said around a mouthful of croissant.

"Glad to hear it, Jake. And thanks again for joining me last minute. And Saturday morning to boot."

Was that Smith-Daniels trying to put a twang on the "to boot"? Jake thought, nodding as he dug into his eggs.

"That said, Jake, I won't keep you long this morning, and I'll cut right to the chase." Smith-Daniels stirred his tea. "When I heard you were no longer going to be at MegaMusic, I suggested Brice reach out to you. I've followed your career for quite some time, and I've always been an admirer of your work."

"Come again?" Jake tilted his head toward him, not quite sure he'd heard him correctly. "You know *my* work?"

"Why is that surprising?" he asked, taking a sip of his tea. "You've been a successful recording artist. You're a hit songwriter—"

Was a hit songwriter, Jake thought bitterly.

"You're a hot commodity, in my humble opinion."

"Well, I'm some kind of commodity." Jake poured some more coffee from the French press. "I wouldn't exactly call it 'hot.'"

"Ah well, what do you attribute that to?" Daniel fixed his gaze on Jake. "What's changed?"

"Hey, I wish I knew. I've been doing the same thing that I've always done. You know, I think a lot has to do with where radio is these days. It's just that pop-country stuff on the charts. Just not the kind of thing I do, you know?"

"Well rewind a bit." He sat up and leaned in. "You said you've been doing the same thing that you've always done. Perhaps that's the problem."

Ah, the same thing that Brice said yesterday.

"Jake, your talent isn't in question," Daniel continued. "There are very few people in Nashville, or anywhere for that matter, who can claim the kind of success you've had. No, I would humbly suggest that maybe your approach to your craft—that, as you said, you're doing the same thing that you've always done—*is* the reason you're not currently enjoying the level of success that you've had in the past."

"Okay, but I'm writing great songs." Jake couldn't help getting a little defensive. "I mean, they're solid tunes."

"Yes, absolutely. You're an A-list songwriter not just in Nashville, but in any city," Daniel said. "Let me give you an example of what I'm talking about. Take, oh, General Motors. Now they've always made high-quality automobiles more or less, right? Every year GM comes out with new models and new looks. New models that incorporate the latest technical advances, trends, safety, and designs in the business, correct?"

"Sure," he said, uncertain where this was going, "but we're talking songwriting."

"Ah, stay with me. So their cars compete and succeed against vehicles made around the world because they keep their ear to the ground. They exhaustively track what the consumers want. They have dozens of design teams that collaborate to vet ideas and then, working together, they set out to build new vehicles year after year."

"True," he said.

"Now, what would happen to their businesses if they stopped constantly evolving their products? If they quit innovating? What if they made cars the same way they've always done, the same way they did fifty years ago? For that matter, the same way they did *five* years ago?"

"Ah well, their cars wouldn't be able to compete." Jake played along, but he could see where Daniel might be going. "Their vehicles' looks and features would feel dated, I guess."

"Ding, ding, ding! Precisely," Daniel exclaimed. "Their talent at building cars, *amazing* cars, wouldn't be in question, but their relevancy in today's market would be highly suspect."

"Okay, you've got my attention, but where would I start? I mean building cars is one thing. What would I do differently as a songwriter?" Jake always liked a straight shooter, and here was a billionaire genius—hell, a damn knight—telling him he needed to do something different.

"Ah, the question I've been waiting for." Daniel smiled and placed his napkin on the table. "When we begin asking questions, then we begin opening ourselves up to new possibilities, don't we? And that's the first step towards doing something differently."

"Let me guess." Jake remembered his conversation with Brice. "Is this where you bring up The Method?"

"Precisely." Daniel lowered his voice a bit and gave Jake a wink. "In the elevator a moment ago, I told you that the real trick in life isn't *having* success, but rather it's *keeping* success. Many people—most people, in fact—*have* success at some point in their lives, but very few people *keep* success."

"Can't argue with that." Hell, he was living proof of it.

"It's not their fault though," Daniel said. "They simply don't have the tools needed in order to stay successful."

"Enter The Method?" Jake interjected, and he couldn't help but feel a little silly.

"Enter The Method." Daniel stood up from the table and gestured for Jake to follow him. "I had to call it something, right? Though 'Enter the Method' sounds like a bad martial arts film." He shook his head and laughed. "At any rate, Jake, the reason I had Brice reach out is that I'm interested in having you as a writer here at The Row."

"Well, thanks, Daniel." Jake followed him back into the expansive studio, and they walked toward another door he hadn't noticed earlier.

"Provided, however, you can free up some of your time, Jake," he said. "I'd like to schedule five writing dates with you and some different members of the team so you can see how we operate, how we work The Method, so to speak. After these five sessions, we can see if we're a good fit for each other."

"Well, the good news is that my schedule is pretty open." Jake shrugged. "The folks over at MegaMusic pretty much quit booking writing appointments for me once they decided not to renew my contract. Hell, I'm all yours."

"Ah, their loss is our gain, perhaps." Daniel raised his finger in the air to punctuate his words as he opened the door and walked into what looked like his private office.

Where the studio room had been open, light, and expansive, Daniel's corner office was warm and supremely comfortable: dark wood tones and overstuffed furniture. Still thoroughly modern, it had an entirely different feel from what Jake had seen thus far. Daniel went behind his desk, and Jake sat opposite him.

Now this is the kind of office you'd expect for a groundbreaking billionaire, Jake thought.

Files and books were neatly stacked on the desk and on furniture around the room. Several computer monitors, really just huge flat-screen televisions, were mounted on the far wall to Jake's left.

"So, Daniel . . . Sir Daniel," Jake said. "What exactly is The Method?"

"Just plain Daniel is fine, Jake." Daniel smiled at him. "I was as blown away as anyone about all that nonsense, but when the Queen of England summons you . . . well, you take a knee." He shifted in his seat and continued. "There's a famous quote from Picasso that always stuck with me. 'All children are born artists. The problem is how to remain artists once we grow up.'"

"One of my favorite Picasso quotes." Jake nodded.

"Yes, it's a good one, and germane to the topic at hand. The question is: how do we grow *into* our creativity as opposed to *out* of it, right? How do we get more creative the older and more experienced we become? It seems as though we would, but more often than not, the opposite is true. Now, I don't believe Picasso was suggesting we're all, say, a Jackson Pollock, destined to do drip paintings in their Montauk studio, sipping on an eighteen-year-old scotch while a beautiful muse prods us on from a Le Corbusier chair . . . Though that doesn't sound half bad!"

Smith-Daniels got up from his desk and approached the vast window of his office. He turned back to Jake.

"What I believe Picasso was getting at was that all of us— whether we're bakers, plumbers, mathematicians, or songwriters— bring artistry to our craft. If we can take Picasso at his word, then it's not a stretch to say what will help one artist stay creative, inspired, relevant, successful, and ultimately happy . . . will also help another artist."

"And we're all artists," Jake chimed in.

"Precisely, Jake, but we're more than that." He clapped his hands together and sat back down at his desk, as though he were going to say something and then reconsidered. "The Method. It's simple really. A set of practices, a way of approaching your craft, your *art* if you will, on a daily basis. I took a deep dive, Jake, looking for commonalities among highly effective people in a wide range of occupations, the business greats we all know."

"Such as?" Jake asked.

"Branson, Welch, Buffet, Musk. Of course, that's easy, but I also looked at the leaders in cutting-edge, niche occupations like gene mapping, nanotechnology, and the creative fields—writers, painters, and musicians like yourself. Individuals who have maintained or increased their level of success over a period of time."

"And you found?"

"That there were a number of exercises these people did that were the same among all of them. We're talking songwriting right now, but I developed The Method to work in any career, regardless of one's line of work."

"Okay, so . . ." He wasn't sure how to ask the question, but Daniel seemed to know.

"The Method is made up of five practices, or routines." He

leaned back in his chair. "So, in each of the five songwriting sessions we're going to schedule, you will be introduced to a new routine in The Method. Simple."

"Does this involve a lot of physical exertion?" Jake rubbed his shoulder gingerly. "Cause it's been awhile since my last Cross-Fit class."

"Ha! No, but you may need to bring a swimsuit to one, if I'm correct," Daniel smiled.

"Uh, what?" Jake waited for him to laugh, but apparently he was serious about the swimsuit.

"Trust, Jake," Daniel winked. "Leap, and the net will appear."

"I'm a little afraid of heights," Jake said. "But what the hell. When do we start?"

"How about Monday? I can have Misha reach out to you later today, and you two can lock down five sessions with our different Row writers."

"Monday is great, Daniel." Jake felt a rush of excitement, but he was oddly also a little nervous. "And do I bring the swimsuit?"

"Ha, no, just bring your guitar, if you'd like, and your A game." Daniel played a little air guitar. "You'll be writing on the first floor with HitCoin."

"'Scuse me?" Jake wasn't sure if he'd heard correctly. Now he didn't keep up with pop music *at all*, but he did know who HitCoin was: the moniker for Brit Kanuka, one of the hottest songwriters in the business. Jamaican-born but grew up in Paris, he was up there with Max Martin, Pharrell, Benny Blanco—you name it. "Does HitCoin know he's writing with me?"

"Yep. I had a feeling you might be available, so last night I took the liberty of calling Brit and asked him if you could join his session Monday. He said sure. He's a fan."

"Huh . . . HitCoin knows who I am?" First, Sir Daniel knows Jake, and now the hottest songwriter in the biz is gonna write with him.

"Yes, Jake." Daniel laughed. "Why does that seem so far-fetched?"

"I mean, it's just that lately I've started feeling... I don't know, irrelevant?" Jake found himself being uncharacteristically honest. "Meeting you, coming here, and now writing with HitCoin. It all seems a bit unreal."

Daniel eyed Jake studiously and put his hands together, only fingertips touching, and then he spoke.

"Jake, let me tell you a story. When I was ten years old, my father—God rest his soul—took me to my first concert. We were there to see the headliner, but it was the opening act," he stood up, walked around to Jake's side of the dark wood desk, and leaned his hip against the corner of it. "The opening act made the biggest impression on me. The music spoke to me in a way that nothing had before. Sure, I was a lad of ten, but it made me want to go home that very instant and start writing songs, which is exactly what I did. It sparked something in me that I didn't know was there. You want to know who that was?"

"Well, sure." *Where is this kid going with this story?*

Daniel gestured at something on the wall behind Jake, and Jake spun his chair around. There, between two bookcases, in a large, gilded frame, was a concert poster. Jake took a breath. He knew the poster immediately. REM at London's Royal Albert Hall with special guest, Jake Stark, complete with original Howard Finster's hand-drawn artwork. And it was signed by Jake.

"Whoa, that's amazing, I . . ." Jake was really at a loss for words, but he found them regardless. "I can't believe you have that poster, Daniel. Now that, that was such a special show. I remember—"

"Thom Yorke from Radiohead came out during REM's encore." Daniel smiled broadly. "I'll never forget it. But, Jake, it was your opening set that really captivated me."

"Wow, that's a strong endorsement, Daniel." Jake felt something akin to pride—a feeling that had been foreign to him as of late. "But REM . . . Radiohead . . . Those are pretty big acts. That said, thank you."

Jake stood up and walked over to the frame, touching it gently.

"And I signed it for you." Jake stared intently at the poster. "Searching the memory banks for that, but coming back empty right now."

"Oh, it was a long time ago, but here's the thing, Jake. In art, in life, in business, we never know who we impact. We never know the influence our work might have on those who come in contact with it." Daniels's tone grew serious. "It is a gift we are given, and it's a responsibility we have as creators to do the best we can do, and to do it for as long as possible. To never let that gift languish. We should always nurture it and continue to grow as creative animals."

"Which I'm guessing brings us full circle back to The Method." Jake felt himself smile and turned away from the poster.

"Yep." Daniel motioned for Jake to follow him out of the office. They walked through the large creative space, over the terrazzo floors, to the elevator doors in the reception area. Daniel pressed the elevator button, and the doors opened almost immediately. They stepped inside.

"So often in life," Daniel turned to Jake, "when some great upheaval, some event happens to us, we think we know what just happened. But more times than not, we don't know. In the moment, that is. It's not until we look back that we see the true impact of events that transpired."

"Meaning?" Jake asked.

"Meaning that I think that MegaMusic not renewing your publishing deal is one of those events. Perhaps you think it's a sign of a declining songwriting career, but I like to think of it as an opportunity for change, for growth, and for success. For—"

"For *keeping* success?" Jake interjected.

"Ha, yes, exactly." He patted Jake on the back as the elevator doors opened, and they walked out into the ground-floor lobby toward the garage. They strode silently until they reached Jake's beat-up old Range Rover and Smith-Daniels's gleaming new Tesla.

"Between now and Monday, Jake, actually throughout these five writes," Daniel fished in his pocket for his key card, "I want you to do the opposite of what you normally do."

"How do you mean?" Jake turned to face him as they both stood behind their vehicles.

"Well, let's focus on work and songwriting right now, but when you're making decisions, I'd like you to consider some contrary action. Do the opposite, perhaps, of what you normally do. Or at least consider it."

"Uh, okay. It's a bit vague, but I get you. Deal." Jake was already taking the request to heart. Where he would have made a joke about Daniel's somewhat odd suggestion, he decided to put that advice into practice and just take it in.

Jake was almost to his car door when Daniel spoke again.

"Oh, and Jake?" That crisp British accent again. "I almost forgot."

"What's that?" Jake looked at Daniel over the hood of his Rover.

"When you were with Brice yesterday, you said you wanted to write the 'greatest song ever'?"

"Well..." He tried to hide his embarrassment and hoped Daniel didn't think he was being silly or egotistical. "What I meant was, I think I still have amazing songs inside of me."

"Ah, that's all well and good, but are you truly interested in writing the greatest song ever? The song that stands the test of time?" Daniel fixed Jake with a stare. "The song that inspires, that emboldens, that impacts lives?"

Again, Jake was tempted to say something smart, but decided to take a little contrary action.

"I wouldn't be here if I didn't want more," he said, "and if I didn't have something great to give." He felt a surge of resolve.

"Ah, that's what I want to hear, Jake." Daniel opened his car door. "Right here, right now, I will tell you, if you follow The Method and truly devote yourself to the process, you will write the greatest song ever. Does that sound good?"

"Daniel," Jake said without a note of sarcasm, "that sounds like a plan."

"Perfect. Well, enjoy your weekend, Jake." Daniel disappeared into his vehicle, and Jake got into his.

Jake pulled the creaking Rover back out of the parking spot and followed the silent Tesla out of the garage and onto Seventeenth Avenue South. It was a brilliant Saturday, and right in the moment, everything seemed brighter—the color of the sky, the green of the leaves, and certainly his mood. There was a song was on the radio, something modern, and Jake looked down at the dial. Somehow his radio had gotten changed to the hit radio station. Reflexively, he went to turn it back to his usual station, but something made him pause.

As he drove, crossing over Wedgewood Drive toward Green Hills, he listened to the song. It was a duet, something super pop and up-tempo. But the melody . . . it was amazing. The melodic accents happened in a fresh unexpected way—something Jake would never have written, but something that he totally loved. By the second verse of the song, he was humming along and playing air drums on the Rover's steering wheel. For the first time in a long time, Jake Stark felt like Jake Stark. He gunned the Rover, and it backfired in protest. The whole vehicle slowed down but kept going.

Not so fast, Jake. You got a long way ahead of you.

INTRO *(in-trō)* *n.* the beginning of the song, which establishes the key, tempo, rhythmic feel, energy, and attitude **||** the foundation, the DNA, the *personality* of the song **||** sets the tone of the entire song and determines what direction the song will take **||** contains the elements that determine whether a song is successful.

Chapter 3

PRACTICE ONE: *CREATIVE COLLABORATION*

For the rest of the weekend, Jake was buzzing. He'd been energized by the meeting. Sir Daniel's enthusiasm—and, quite honestly, his belief in Jake's potential to still write hits—was something Jake realized now that he really needed to hear and to feel. Jake actually found himself practicing contrary actions and doing the opposite of what he was normally inclined to do. He'd left the radio in the old Rover to the pop music station and found that he liked what he heard. It was fresh and exciting, and the productions—the way the songs were recorded and sounded—were amazing.

He'd also gotten his lazy butt up when he'd wanted to stay in bed Sunday morning and went with Sarah and Mac for their weekly hike in Percy Warner Park. It had been a beautiful day, and it was nice to spend some time outdoors with his son. Jake realized how quickly Mac was growing up; he needed to be more present in his son's life. Later, on Sunday afternoon while listening to music outside on his porch, Jake decided—with more than a bit of hesitation but practicing contrary action—to listen to the MP3 of the song Cal's daughter had written. Amazingly, it was good! The song wasn't perfect. It was rough in spots, but the chorus, the hook of the song, was undeniable. This young woman was talented.

Wow, Jake thought. *I was nowhere near as good a writer when I was that age. I was terrible, in fact.*

Jake responded to Cal's email and offered to have coffee with his daughter at some point over the next couple of weeks. He'd be happy to give her some pointers and some encouragement. Who knows? Maybe they could get together and work on a song . . .

Contrary action indeed.

On Monday morning, once again, at 7:30 a.m. sharp, Jake's alarm went off to the familiar hand-picked guitar part of Nilsson's "Everybody's Talkin'." Jake lay in bed and thought about how many mornings he must have heard that song. A thousand? More? Then, instead of lying on the couch, drinking coffee, and watching ESPN all morning, Jake threw on some shorts and rode his bike to (drum roll . . .) the gym. Jake hadn't been in ages.

This contrary action stuff is gonna kill me, Jake thought as he huffed along on the treadmill.

After an hour or so at the gym, Jake came back to the house, took a shower, and by 9:30 a.m. was headed to The Row. He made a quick detour to Bongo Java for some coffee and a bite and was soon driving down Music Row on Seventeenth Avenue South.

Jake could feel his nerves building the closer he got to The Row. HitCoin, one of the top songwriters in the world, was about to become his writing partner for the day. Jake knew he needed to be on top of his game.

He still couldn't believe the series of events that had happened since last week. He'd been let go by his publisher, met with a knighted billionaire in his twenties, and most surprisingly he'd gone to the gym. Anything could happen.

As Jake pulled his SUV into The Row's ultramodern building, his phone lit up with a text from an LA area code: 310.

> Jake, Brit here. We're on the first floor in Studio A. Looking forward to our write.

Jake hopped out of the Rover and grabbed his guitar from the backseat. As he began walking through the parking garage to the lobby door, he saw Misha exiting a gleaming black Audi.

"Good morning, Misha!" He felt uncharacteristically good for a Monday morning. "You ready to tackle Monday?"

"Jake, good morning." Misha looked radiant way too early. "What a brilliant day, right?"

"That it is, Misha," he said as he opened the door to the lobby.

"I'm so excited to be working with you and Brit today." Misha stepped into the lobby, and he followed.

"Oh, uh . . . me too. We're gonna get a good one. I can feel it," Jake said. He was taken aback that Misha was joining them. He'd been under the impression that it was just going to be a two-way write with HitCoin and him. Now, it was going to be a three-way write, which Jake didn't usually do. Why split the song—and the royalties—three ways? He never really needed more than one other person to write a song. At that moment, walking into the lobby, Jake started to question everything he had been doing and thinking the past few days. *Does Sir Kid think I need help writing with HitCoin? Do they think I'm a has-been? I'm not enough?*

"I agree, Jake." Misha jarred him from his thoughts as they entered the elevator.

Jake pushed the button for the first floor, but just as the elevator door was about to close, a hand shot through the gap, causing the door to open again.

"Hold that elevator," a disembodied British voice rang out from the lobby.

The door opened to reveal a short young man with reddish hair wearing a sloppy outfit—an oversized Beastie Boys T-shirt and cargo shorts. Jake was annoyed that this guy had stopped their car abruptly, and then it hit him, who this person was.

"Ed, how are you?" Misha squealed. "Oh my god, why didn't you tell me you were in town? You're in trouble." She gave the incoming guy a huge bear hug.

Jake couldn't believe it. The *guy* was Ed Sheeran.

"Meesh, I'm so sorry, I'm just in town for the day to write with Daniel," he said as he hit the button for the fifth floor. "Then I'm right back up to New York tonight. I would so like to hang out though."

"It's okay, love. We'll get together next time." Misha stepped back and turned toward Jake. "Oh, Ed, I want you to meet Jake Stark. Excellent writer, I might add. I'm working with Jake and Brit today."

"Pleasure to meet you, Jake," Ed-friggin'-Sheeran said to Jake Stark. "You're in for an amazing write. Brit's okay, but Misha is an insane writer."

"Guess I gotta bring my A game today," Jake said, and Ed and Misha laughed. Jake thought about cracking a joke about "The A Team," but decided against it.

"Absolutely, mate," Ed said as the elevator door opened to the first floor. "Have a good one, and Misha, I promise to let you know next time I'm in town."

Ed and Misha hugged quickly, and Jake gave a small wave to Ed as the doors to the elevator silently closed.

"Well, that was Ed Sheeran," Jake deadpanned.

"Oh, he's here all the time," Misha said as she motioned for Jake to follow her down the sleek hallway that stretched out before them. "He's quite a nuisance, really."

"Ha, he seems cool."

"He's the best." They came to a door with a large A on it at the end of the hallway. She knocked gently and opened the door. "The best talent."

As the door opened, natural light flooded into the dimly lit hallway. Immediately Jake saw that Studio A was actually the whole back half of the first floor. It was a gleaming white room with terrazzo floors, just like the ones on the fifth floor. *Kilim* rugs covered the floor, and comfortable but modern furniture surrounded a control desk covered with the usual recording equipment and a computer monitor. By the desk stood Brit Kanuka.

"Ah, *bonjour*, Misha! Jake, it's a pleasure to meet you." Brit walked over to them as he spoke. Jake could clearly hear the French accent punctuated by a touch of a Jamaican one, but if you didn't know better, you'd say he was a hip-hop producer from New Orleans.

He was wearing Adidas sweatpants, a vintage Gucci T-shirt, Havaianas flip-flops, and a New Orleans Saints baseball cap. What smelled like sandalwood incense burned on the edge of the desk.

"Brit, so good to have you back from LA." Misha threw her arms around him in a hug. "We've missed you."

"Good to be back, Misha." Brit turned to Jake. "And you must be the famous Jake Stark."

"Famous? I don't know about that." Jake shook Brit's hand. "But I would be Jake Stark."

"Well, I can tell you that you have a fan in Daniel Smith-Daniels," said Brit. "And that counts for something."

"Oh, well, you know, he flatters me," Jake said. "Nice to know that at least someone out there remembers the music."

"I think more than just one person. But since we're talking about music, how about we make some?" Brit slapped his hands together and turned to the computer monitor.

Jake and Misha took their places on the sofa behind Brit. Jake grabbed his acoustic guitar from its case and opened up his laptop on the coffee table. Misha put her iPad on the coffee table, as well. For the next ten minutes or so, the three songwriters just caught up and got to know one another. They talked food, travel, gossip, and of course, music. Finally, Brit asked the question that always popped up at some point in the beginning of a songwriting session.

"What do we want to work on today?"

For big songwriting sessions, Jake would always pregame the day before and would have a couple of song ideas to kick off the session. He was used to being the person with the ideas in the room, doing the heavy lifting, so to speak. Today was no exception, and since Jake had been listening to the pop radio station, *and* he was writing with a songwriter with massive pop hits, he had come up with a few melodies to get them started. Jake was just about to say he had an idea or two when Misha spoke.

"Well, I have something that I started humming on the way to the studio this morning." She sat forward on the edge of the couch, not the least bit shy. "I don't know what the chords would be, but it goes something like this."

Going into today, Jake had had the idea this session was going to be an audition of sorts for him as a potential Row writer. Now, Misha had joined the session, and here she was introducing one of her ideas. Jake was fully prepared not to like whatever it was that Misha was about to sing, but from the second the notes escaped her lips, he was hooked. It was instantly memorable and infectious. The tune had a lilting melody with a bit of a Jamaican swagger. Like something Rhianna might sing.

"Eh, ya oh, hanging on the edge of your kiss, your lips, so perilous..." Misha sang low but with confidence.

"I love it. Brilliant!" Brit blurted out, and began quickly finding the chords that went under the melody of what Misha was singing.

In minutes, the two of them were off to the races, and Jake was still standing at the starting line, holding on to the melodies of the song ideas he had prepared. For the first time ever in a songwriting session, he felt like *he* was the one not doing the work. Brit even started adding some beats to the chords. At that moment, Jake was about to disconnect because, quite honestly, this was new and uncomfortable. For the first time in a long time, a song was happening in a session, and it didn't start with him. Add to that he hadn't contributed a thing to the quickly developing idea.

Jake was about to say he thought the melody could be stronger or in some way diminish the idea, but then he heard Daniel's voice in his head. *Take contrary action, Jake.* That was all Jake needed.

"Misha, it's really great, and Brit, I dig starting on the minor chord." Jake stood up and walked to an upright piano. "How about... Misha start the melody right on the downbeat of the chorus instead

THE GREATEST SONG | 53

of waiting. Then repeat 'perilous' like this at the end of the chorus," Jake sang his idea.

"Oh, I love that!" Misha called back. "It makes the chorus pop a lot harder."

"Exactly," Brit said. "And how about if I build a swell like this." He took a moment and built the musical piece on the computer. He hit PLAY, and Misha began singing along.

When Misha got to the end of the chorus and repeated "perilous" the way Jake had sung it . . . well, it was epic.

"Oh, hell yes," Brit whooped. "Hit dance!"

And with that, Brit got up from his chair and began doing a silly old-school break dance—something Vanilla Ice would have been embarrassed to do. Misha and Jake started clapping along, and Jake might have done a little beat box under his breath. It was exhilarating though. That hair-standing-up-on-the-back-of-your-neck excitement about an idea that Jake hadn't felt in . . . well, he couldn't remember how long.

"Oh, this is a keeper, everyone," Brit said, a little out of breath as he sat back down at his desk. "Okay, I'm going to flesh out the track a little more here on the chorus and the post chorus. Misha, you and Jake start working on the verse."

"Sounds good, Brit." Misha said and turned to Jake. "Where do you think the verse should go? Keep the same chord progression?"

"Yeah, but how about we just stay on each chord twice as long, so the verse feels linear, more static." Jake picked up his trusty '57 Gibson J-45 acoustic guitar and started finger-picking a part through the minor chord progression.

"Oh, that's a dope part. How about this?" Misha brushed her hair behind her ears and began to hum a bit.

"Love that, Misha," Brit said, turning his head away from the computer monitor where he was building the musical bed of the song. "Get those words now. I would help, but I'm shite at lyrics."

"Walls of my will are caving in . . ." Jake singing some words to the melody Misha had been humming. "It's dangerous letting us begin . . ."

"Oh, that's rad," Misha said, typing lyrics into her iPad.

For the next three hours—and as many cups of coffee—they kept writing. Jake, Brit, and Misha threw ideas at each other, each making the song better than if they had written it on their own. Jake couldn't remember having a better time or a song being more effortlessly written than what they had that day. No egos and no agendas other than doing great work and helping each other do it. They had started around 10:30 a.m., and by 2:45 p.m., they had a finished song with a good musical track and vocals recorded by Misha. It sounded like a song that could be cut by anyone from Olivia Rodrigo to SZA to Carrie Underwood. As they were congratulating each other on a good session and packing up their stuff to leave Studio A, Brit leaned over to Jake.

"Mate, wanna join me for a walk? We can grab a late lunch at Taco Amigo, or maybe a coffee? Your call."

Jake was about to say he needed to be somewhere, but then realized he didn't. *Contrary action.*

"Uh, yeah, that sounds great. Just let me throw my guitar in my truck, and I'll be good."

The three of them headed out of the studio. Once down the elevator and in the garage, Misha hugged Jake and Brit goodbye— she was zipping off to another songwriting session across town. Jake and Brit walked out of the garage as Misha's Audi whipped past them, down Seventeenth Avenue South, and out of sight. It was a gorgeous spring Monday in Nashville. Jake and Brit had the sidewalk and street to themselves as they walked the few blocks down to the restaurant.

"Great time today, Brit," Jake said. "Had a blast, and our song is killer."

"It's a really strong one. There are a lot of artists who can cut that track," Brit replied in his cool French/Jamaican accent.

"We'll have to do it again," Jake said as they got to Edgehill Drive.

"Absolutely, mate." Brit pressed the walk button at the light. "I'm glad you could join us last minute."

"Oh, hell yes, me too," Jake said.

"So . . ." Brit waited a beat. "So, I know Daniel—"

"Sir Daniel?" Jake cut in.

"Ha, yeah, *Sir* Daniel. It is crazy he's a knight of the British Realm." Brit smiled. "So Sir Daniel, he mentioned The Method to you, right?"

"Oh yeah, still kinda shrouded in mystery," Jake said. "We'll see when I start finding out what it's all about."

"Mate, we've been doing the first step in The Method all day." Brit snapped his fingers. "The first step, the first *practice*, of The Method is collaboration. Creative collaboration."

"Uh, okay . . . Well, step one is done," Jake said, and dusted his hands together, blackjack-dealer style.

"Ah, but no . . . really you're just starting," Brit continued. "Today isn't the first time you've written a song with someone. It's not the first time you've collaborated."

"Well, no," Jake agreed.

"Real collaboration, creative collaboration, is when you not only work with others to create something or solve a problem, but you actually allow them to bring their skill set to the table, to have input in the collaboration. You allow them—"

"To be heard?" Jake took a stab at it. He was thinking of the session that he'd just left and how he hadn't wanted to listen to Misha's idea. After all, he'd had a couple of ideas that he thought were winners, and he'd wanted to tune out when Misha beat him to the punch. He'd wanted to show how good his idea was, and surely Misha's idea wasn't as good as his. After all, he was Jake Stark. Right.

"Exactly!" Brit let out a hoot. "Most of us, when we work with others, aren't really there to truly collaborate. We're there to exert our will on a situation, right? Show everyone else how good we are and get our ideas heard and used. And get the credit in the process. But what really happens is we block out the truly great ideas. We're not listening to someone's idea. We're thinking about what we're about to say. It's really not collaboration at all. Our being in that kind of false collaborative environment is more an act of compliance than one of willingness."

"Yeah, I can relate." Jake was struck by the wisdom of this guy. *How old is he? Twenty-seven . . . twenty-eight? Same age as Sir Daniel? Definitely didn't expect to be having this kind of conversation with him.*

"Jake, when I started out about ten years ago, I thought every idea I had was amazing and everyone else's were shite—or suspect, at the very least. When I worked with others, it was all about me and my ideas, and having my ideas used over other people's, regardless of whether those ideas were better than mine. And honestly, I had no idea if their idea was better than mine because I would barely listen to what anyone else was suggesting. I only had one agenda: 'Listen to what I've got.' The problem was that I was having some success despite myself, so I thought what I was doing, how I was proceeding, was acceptable."

"I've built a career working like that." Jake let out a quiet laugh and realized that was pretty much how he'd conducted himself his entire adult life, not only in work, but also in his relationship with Sarah.

"Right? You know a wise old friend told me I really needed to check my ego, and that's especially true in songwriting. But he had a great phrase. 'My ego is not my amigo,'" Brit said, and laughed out loud.

"That's great, I'm stealing that." Jake slapped his hands together.

"But at some point, I just hit a wall. I'd reached a level of success that I couldn't exceed, or so I thought. At best, I just kind of pla-teaued, and at worst, well, my work wasn't as good as it had been. Interestingly enough, that's right about the time I met Daniel."

"In London?" Jake asked and thought how many lives this guy had touched.

"At the *BRIT Awards.*" Brit nodded. "We ended up meeting for breakfast a few days later, and Sir Daniel—actually, just Daniel, he hadn't been knighted at that point—he asked me to be the first signing of The Row. Funny, people here think it's 'The Row' after Music Row, but the first office was on Saville Row in London. That's really where the name comes from. The idea being that the songs written at The Row are bespoke, tailor-made, like the elegant clothes on Saville Row."

"Oh, that's cool," Jake said. "You can drop some coin on clothes on Saville Row."

"Ha, obscene amounts of money on clothes." Brit laughed and stopped as they stood on the corner at Taco Amigo.

"So this is right about the time your career skyrocketed, right?" Jake said, not missing the irony of the restaurant's name. "I remember like three years ago—"

"Yeah, it's been about that long."

"You were everywhere. I mean . . . you still are. It seemed like you had cowritten everything on the charts."

"Well, what Daniel had to say to me at our meeting and subsequent meetings after that really made a lot of sense. The Method, really."

"I was waiting for that." Jake squinted in the sun.

"It's been a game-changer for me, and it's simple. Collaborate as much as you can. Surround yourself with talented people who bring skill sets to the table that you don't have, or someone whose skills are stronger than yours. Set your ego and agendas to the side, and listen to everyone's ideas. *Really* listen. It's all about the song, the finished product. Not about you."

"Yeah, of course," Jake said, "but it's easy to get wrapped up in who's contributing the most when you're working on something."

"I hear you, but when I quit thinking of what I was or wasn't getting and focused on the song only . . . well, that's when my career started blowing up."

"You really think that made all the difference?" Jake wasn't doubting, just trying to understand.

"Before I started working The Method, I wrote most everything myself, or maybe I worked with one other person," Brit said. "And if I did work with three or more on something, I sabotaged it by impressing my ideas on the song, even if that wasn't the best direction to go. But when I served the song and not myself—practiced real creative collaboration—the hits started coming… and coming. And I made more money."

"Better to have 25 percent of a worldwide hit than 100 percent of a song that goes nowhere." Jake had plenty of the latter lately.

"Exactly!" Brit opened the door to Taco Amigo. "And to be known as being generous—someone people want to collaborate with. You know, it becomes a self-fulfilling prophecy. You get to work with people because they think you're going to bring the hit."

"You got the hit juice," Jake said. He motioned for a table for two, and he and Brit began following the host there.

"Right?" Brit laughed as he slid into the booth. "You end up writing with all the best people, and if you keep practicing not just collaboration, but *creative* collaboration as outlined in The Method, well, there's just no end to your success."

Brit turned his attention to the waiter who had approached the table. "Sir, if I'm correct, it's Margarita Monday. My friend and I would like two Casamigos margaritas, por favor." Brit motioned to Jake. "Good with you?"

"What the heck. It's a Monday!" Jake said, although he usually didn't have a drink before dinner. "It's not like it's 'perilous' or anything. Maybe an order of guacamole too, please?"

As the waiter headed back toward the bar, Brit circled back to their conversation. "Now more than ever, we're competing against teams of people, and it's every industry, not just songwriting. Not only are the most successful people immensely talented at their craft, but they're also truly genius in their ability to surround themselves with talented people."

"And they allow those people to do their jobs." Jake thought about the crazy successful producer Max Martin who is surrounded by a talented group of collaborators. "It's all about the long play, isn't it? Take less, get more."

"You got it." Brit slapped his hands together. "And also, there's the value-added part of the equation. When you practice creative collaboration, you become a better writer. You pick up chord progressions, melodies, production ideas that you would have never been exposed to had you not been in that session."

"Like today," Jake said, "I would have never come up with a melody like the one Misha started. It was just so fresh. Oh, and the chords underneath the chorus—what you came up with. I would have never done something with those seventh chords. It's just not my background."

"And guess what?" Brit put his napkin in his lap. "The next session you're in, I assure you that you're going to try and introduce those chords somehow into the song you're writing that day."

"Ha, guilty. You know I am."

They settled into a comfortable silence, and Jake thought about the opportunities he might've missed by dismissing real creative collaboration in the past. He came back to the present when their waiter set down chips, guacamole, and the margaritas. Brit picked up his drink and held it toward Jake in a toast.

"Here's to our song, and here's to taking it to the next level."

"Here, here!" said Jake.

The late lunch went great as Jake and Brit got to know each other better. At one point, Jake's old publisher, Chuck Lane, from MegaMusic came by their table. Chuck clearly knew who Brit was, and Jake could see he was impressed.

Ah, what a difference a week can make, Jake thought as he scooped up the last bit of guacamole in the serving bowl, and, by this time, the tequila had begun to work its sultry magic. The evening sun was slanting through the windows of the restaurant, and Jake Stark just had to smile.

RULES FOR CREATIVE COLLABORATION

1. Take less, get more. The long play in business, and in life, is fostering long-term relationships by conducting yourself in a fair and equitable way. Be generous in credit and ownership. When people see that you are concerned with the finished product and not yourself, they will want to work with you again. This pays the biggest dividends down the road.

2. Be prepared, and be prepared to not use any of the ideas you have at the ready.

3. Remain open to all ideas in the collaborative environment. Really listen to your collaborators. It's not about getting your own ideas across, but rather discovering which ideas are best. Don't micromanage. Despite our best efforts, when we try to control a collaborative session, it often ends up being less productive than if we had allowed it to flow naturally.

4. Check your ego at the door. Remember, in a collaboration, "My ego is not my amigo."

5. Surround yourself with people who bring a skill set that is different from and, hopefully, exceeds your own. You only grow by being around others who challenge you to get better.

Chapter 4

PRACTICE TWO: *FILLING THE WELL*

The next morning, when Jake got back home from the gym (yes, two days in a row to the gym, a record for Jake), there was a text from Misha.

> Jake, I checked your Google calendar, and it looks like you're open this Friday. Can I book you with The Professor? You probably know her as Kate Boom. 9 a.m., second floor at The Row. Oh, and I can't quit singing 'Perilous'! We're going to get this one cut, I just know it!

Jake did a double take at his phone. He couldn't believe it. First, he wrote yesterday with Brit Kanuka, arguably the hottest writer in pop music—hell, any kind of music, for that matter—and now he was gonna write with Kate Boom, or Professor Boom, as she was known as a producer. It simply didn't get any cooler than Kate Boom. Everyone from Kacey Musgraves to Lady Gaga to Harry Styles had worked with her, all to stunning success. Not only was she a gifted pianist and producer, but she was also known to be like a genius-level thinker. Jake immediately texted back with an all caps:

> HELLZ YES!

"Oh yeah, baby!" Jake let out a yelp as he walked to his bedroom. He started singing one of Kacey Musgraves's Kate Boom–penned songs as he disappeared into the steam of the shower stall.

"Okay, what's going on in here?" Suddenly, Sarah's voice happily joined in on the chorus. She put her nose against the fogged-up glass of the stall.

"Hey, babe," Jake said as he opened the door of the shower and gave her a kiss. "I'm just excited is all. Just thinking about the write I told you about from yesterday and the one at the end of the week."

"Oh yay! Who is it?" Sarah was all smiles.

"Kate Boom, she's this amazing—"

"Oh, come on, Jake." Sarah looked radiant in the fog of the bathroom. "I know who Kate Boom is. She's on fire!"

"Yes, she is, and your man is writing with her." Jake turned off the shower, and Sarah grabbed a towel for him.

"You know, it's good to see excitement about writing in your eyes again." Sarah leaned back on the basin and smiled at Jake. "I think whatever you're up to agrees with you."

"Me too, babe. Me too." Jake dried off and then grabbed Sarah's hand. "Let me tell you more about it in my office."

"I would like that very much." Sarah followed Jake out of the bathroom.

"Right this way, babe. Right this way."

Over the next few days, Jake worked with some of his regular go-to writers, people he'd written with for years. That was the way it worked in Nashville: you found a group of people you just clicked with creatively and personally. They were great hangs, and if you got a killer song that day, well, that was just a bonus.

This week, though, it wasn't just business as usual with his regular writes. After Monday's session with Brit and Misha, he'd decided to take a different approach to his collaborations on Tuesday and Thursday. Instead of coming in and immediately trying to run the show with a title idea or a melody, he'd let his cowriter take the lead. Talk about practicing contrary action! It wasn't easy, but the songs they wrote? Are you kidding? They were the best things they'd written together in who knows how many years. Just listening and truly being a creative partner had changed everything.

On Thursday evening, Jake met up with Cal's daughter in East Nashville at Barista Parlor coffee shop. She was great, super smart, and chomping at the bit to carve out her own place in Nashville songwriter history. She and Jake made plans to write the following Tuesday.

Friday morning started as usual with a little Harry Nilsson, and then Jake was off to The Row to write with Professor Boom. *The names in my business,* he thought. *Professor Boom.*

When Jake arrived, there was no Ed Sheeran in the elevator, but Jake did have one of his songs going through his head as he got off on the second floor. He'd been listening to the pop station since this crazy week had started with his meeting with Sir Daniel. As opposed to the first floor of The Row, with its dimly lit hallway and studio doors, the second floor of The Row was alive with people and energy. This was clearly where all the business administration of the publishing company was done. But instead of cubicles housing people crunching numbers, the second floor was an entirely open plan. It was a cool hang area with funky couches, long communal tables, a ping-pong table, retro video games, and plenty of little workspaces where men and women spoke with one another as they went about the business of tracking song publishing money. Jake stood there with his guitar case, just taking it in. Then he stopped somebody as they zipped by on one of those two-wheeled hover boards.

"Excuse me." Jake tapped the guy lightly on his shoulder as he whisked by. "Can you tell me where Kate Boom is?"

"Professor?" The guy didn't look back at Jake but motioned with his arm. "She's in the back on the left."

When Jake looked beyond all the activity on the floor, he noticed for the first time a white door against the back wall. He began to navigate the room, past people drinking cappuccinos (oat milk, if Jake had to guess) from the barista stand on the far left wall. As he approached the door, the heavy thumping of bass grew louder and louder. He could also see glittering gold lettering on the door. When he got closer, he could make out what it said: "Professor Boom."

Ha, Jake thought. *Either she doesn't take herself seriously at all, or she takes herself way too seriously.*

Jake knocked on the door, but the music didn't stop and no one answered. He knocked a little louder. Still no answer, so he cracked the door open a little. Good God, the sound—the level of the music playing was crazy loud. But it sounded amazing. Something like R&B mixed with a little bit of EDM; it was nothing that Jake recognized.

Kate Boom sat in a Herman Miller Aeron chair with her head down, eyes closed, rocking to the music, her short, dark curls bouncing to the rhythm. Jake had seen photos of Kate Boom before, but in person, she was magnetic. She sat in front of the typical studio setup: computer monitor playing back the session with a piano keyboard and other recording gear at her fingertips. What was not typical were all the books and magazines that covered every square inch of available table space. The floor was covered in stacked printouts to the point where you would have to move ninja-like to navigate the room without knocking something over. Jake cleared his throat.

"Uh, excuse me." He spoke loudly over the music, but it didn't get Kate's attention. "Hello, Ms. Boom."

And at that, Kate Boom looked up and flashed a huge, glowing smile. She hit the space bar on her computer keyboard, and the music stopped.

"Jake Stark, yes?" She stood up and stepped toward him, moving deftly around the stacked papers.

THE GREATEST SONG | 67

"Why, yes, that would be me." Jake flashed her his biggest smile. He extended his hand, but Kate Boom went right in for a hug.

"Such a pleasure to meet you, Jake. Welcome, and pardon the mess." Kate stepped back and motioned toward the couch where, incredibly, there was some room for him to sit down.

Jake made his way to the couch and set his guitar case on top of a stack of papers.

"The pleasure is mine. I've been a fan of your writing and your production for a while." He opened the case up and pulled out his trusty J-45 Gibson acoustic.

"Oh, she's beautiful!" Kate said as she sat back down at the computer desk and leaned forward to look at Jake's guitar. "Is that a '57 J-45?"

"Uh, yeah." Jake couldn't believe she got it right just by looking. You had to know *a lot* about guitars to know the year, especially on a guitar as old as this. "My uncle gave it to me when I got my first record deal way back when."

"May I?" said Kate, raising her eyebrows and gesturing toward the guitar.

"Of course." Jake handed the acoustic to Kate.

"It's gorgeous!" She strummed a few chords gently.

Now Jake had been playing music a long time and had heard some of the best. He was not an easily impressed person when it came to guitar playing, but when Kate really dug into his guitar, he could tell his trusty J-45 was in the hands of an accomplished player. After strumming a bit and getting a feel for the neck, Kate launched into a difficult finger-picked blues song that would have made Mississippi John Hurt envious. Her playing was incredible. Then she played a bit of the classical song "Maleguena" up high on the neck, but at double time, like something Michael Hedges would have played.

"Brilliant guitar, Jake." Kate suddenly stopped and handed the J-45 back to him.

Jake took it, his mouth ajar.

"Holy crap! Where did that come from?" He blew on the fretboard of the guitar as if to cool it off. "You're a monster. An accomplished pianist *and* a smoking guitar player?"

"Oh, that?" Kate said and waved her hand. "That's just messing around."

"But where did you learn to play like that? That's not music school stuff." Jake was still blown away.

"Well, I grew up in Chicago, and my father is a blues musician. He's played guitar with Howlin' Wolf, Muddy Waters, Koko Taylor . . . Oh, and I went to Julliard." Kate tapped the side of her head.

"Well, that is quite a pedigree! So cool. I wish I could play my own guitar like that."

"Oh, I'm sure you're no slouch." Kate fiddled with her computer keyboard and pulled up a fresh recording session on her computer. "So, Jake, what do you want to work on?"

"A hit song, Kate. How about that?" he said. "Let's just go ahead and set that bar high."

"I love it." Kate turned to him. "But before we go there, let me ask you something."

"Fire away," Jake said.

"Can you tell me any of the songs in the Top 10 on the Top 40 chart?" Kate raised an eyebrow.

"Hmmmm . . . that's a good question. I have no earthly idea. I mean there's a lot of crap, I know." Jake defaulted to his usual position on the state of the music industry, puzzled about where Kate was going.

"Ah, well, how about an easy one? How about something in the Top 10 on the country chart?" Kate raised an eyebrow again and cocked her head. "That's your wheelhouse, right? What you usually write for?"

"Oh, don't get me started on Country Hit radio. It's the worst. That bro country?" Jake was getting worked up and ready to hop up on his soapbox. "Uh, but yes, that's most of the songs I write, country ones. But isn't there a Keith Urban song that's up there?"

"Ha, that's a pretty good guess considering he always has songs out, and hit ones. But no, there's not currently an Urban song in the Top 10 right now, or anywhere in the country charts, for that matter."

"So where you going with this, Kate Boom?" He still didn't quite follow what Kate might be getting at. This wasn't the way you usually started out a session.

"Oh, I'm just trying to get a sense of where you are," Kate said. "And sorry for the quiz, Jake. I'm a bit of a data junkie. I pore over the charts and news in the music business. I consume new music all the time. Twenty-four-seven. It's just a part of what we call filling the well."

"Ah, that's why they call you The Professor?" Jake said and strummed a chord on the guitar.

"Yes, that's why they put that ridiculous name on my door. Sounds so silly, but I secretly like it." Kate let out a laugh, and she pulled her legs up in the chair.

"So what's with this 'filling the well'?" Jake asked.

"Think of your creativity as a contained well," she said, "like one in the ground, but this one..." Kate tapped her chest. "This one is inside, and it's finite. Meaning it only contains what you put in."

"Yeah, okay. I can grasp the concept," Jake said, putting his finger to his lips.

"And all the things that feed our creativity, they come from this well. All our experiences—the music we listen to, our lives, growing up, our first love, our hurt, our pain, our first car, everything . . . It all goes into the well."

"Makes sense." Jake could feel himself getting swept up in her excitement.

"When we create, we pull from that well. We draw upon it, like we're getting buckets of water out. Or better yet, it's like a bank account, and we're making withdrawals, and we keep making withdrawals. When we experience, listen, learn, and consume, we fill the well. And it's incumbent upon us to ensure that our efforts to fill the well outpace our withdrawals." Kate was in her element, now staring intently at him.

"Of course, your deposits have to exceed your withdrawals," he said. "Otherwise, you get overdrawn, and there's nothing left."

"Bingo." Kate clapped her hands together. "And you can't give what you don't have. Or put another way, if you're not being inspired, then you're not going to be able to inspire!"

"Ah, let me guess." Jake started putting the pieces together. "Filling the well. It's the second practice in The Method?"

"Who says songwriters aren't sharp?" Kate laughed. "Yes, it is, or at least, it's the second practice to which I believe you've been introduced. Really, though, it all comes back to what Daniel means when he talks about keeping success. Most people in every profession just get to a point in their lives when they quit learning, growing, and experiencing new things. The sad thing is that for most people, that's right after college or secondary school, sometime in their mid-twenties. Songwriters are no different."

"How do you mean?" Jake was no longer sure if he was following her.

"Well, tell me how many musicians or bands have that first great album, and then everything after that isn't inspired? It's just not as good."

"You mean they suck after they have that big first album?" Jake asked, thinking a little bit about his own recording career.

"That's harsh, but yeah." Kate got up from her chair and walked over to a bowl of almonds on the side table next to the couch. "They had their whole life to make that first album. They drew everything good from the well, and then when they went back, well . . . there was nothing left. At some point, they quit seeking out new inspiration."

"Yeah." Jake nodded. "You ask most people who their favorite band is, and they invariably say somebody they used to listen to in college."

"So, Jake, part of filling the well, or dwelling in the well, as I like to say—" Kate came back to her chair.

"Dwell in the well. I see what you did there."

"Part of it is always listening to new music. Seeking it out. Exploring for the next thing that just blows you away. You go down the rabbit hole on Spotify, YouTube, listening to different radio stations, and without fail, you end up being inspired." Kate was talking so fast she was almost out of breath.

"Sure, that makes sense. And yes, I could do more of that." Jake thought about how he'd been listening to the pop station as of late but, in general, didn't give any new music a chance.

"Yeah, by listening to and studying the new things created in any given field, you know what you're up against. It's amazing how many struggling songwriters I speak to don't listen to any new music. They turn their noses up at it."

"Crazy," Jake said, and realized she could be talking about him.

"And then they wonder why they're not getting cuts and having success. You know, I think it's because their egos won't let them open themselves up to what's going on around them. Then they spin their wheels spitting out music that isn't competitive."

"My ego is not my amigo," said Jake, stealing Brit's line, and he couldn't help but wonder if Kate was speaking in generalities or directly at him.

"Ah, I love that. Yes. Check your ego at the door, because how can you compete if you don't know what you're competing against?" Kate slapped her hand down on the arm of the Aeron chair. "Ouch, that hurt!"

"Amen to that." Jake wondered if he was convincing. "Don't break your hand before we get to write a song, Kate."

"Oh, I'm fine—it's padded! And as I said, that's just part of filling the well," she said. "Tell me, who is the current head of Sony Publishing or Warner Brothers Records? Or name me some of the top label heads here in Nashville or Los Angeles."

Jake was stumped again, but at least he could think of his old publisher at MegaMusic.

"Uh, how about Chuck Lane?"

"Well, somebody other than your old publisher," she said.

Oh, she was good, The Professor.

"Jake, I have a friend in Chicago, Dan Smythe. Perhaps you've heard of him?" Jake shook his head. "Well, he's one of the most successful restauranteurs in the city. He has four places, one of which, Bird and Butcher, is a Michelin Star, James Beard award-winning restaurant, and he's opening a fifth. Now Dan is someone who, if he chose to, could just sit back and count his money. You know, take it easy."

"Yeah, of course," he said. "I've heard of Bird and Butcher."

"It's on the Food Network all the time. Dan could rest on his laurels, so to speak, but the opposite is true. If he's not in one of his kitchens—sleeves rolled, slinging hash—then he's out at his competitors' places, checking out what they're doing right and what they're doing wrong. He's always doing recon."

"That's pretty industrious." Now he got where Kate was going. "Scouting the other team, so to speak."

"Exactly. And the more you fill the well with inspiration, but also knowledge about music and the music industry, the better the chances are you're going to be able to connect the dots—the dots to not only a hit song, but also the dots to getting that hit into the right hands. If you know who is working and where they're working, you're able to leverage those friendships and connections."

"You're talking about the trades like *Billboard* and *MusicRow, R&R*?" he said.

"Right. All of them tell you what's happening on the charts, but they also tell you how the business is shifting and where the players are moving from label to label, publisher to publisher."

Kate was interrupted by a knock at the door.

"C'mon in," she called.

A young woman, arms filled with a bag containing lunch from a Thai place down the street, pushed open the door with her shoulder.

"Praise the lord," said Kate, "I was starving! I hope you like Thai food, Jake."

THE GREATEST SONG | 73

"It's my favorite, and yeah, I'm famished," Jake told her and rubbed his hands together.

Kate and Jake scarfed down the food and then jumped into writing a song. Throughout the session, Kate continually consulted different tracks for reference and was keen about knowing who was looking for songs and what kind of songs they were looking for. It was refreshing as hell for Jake, who, as a rule, avoided ever admitting where inspiration might have come from. The song they worked on had a great melodic piano hook that Kate played into Pro Tools, the computer program they were using to record. She built a great drum track to support the piano. Jake sang a vocal melody that just popped into his head as Kate played the piano.

"I miss you more . . . I miss you more . . ." Jake sang over the propulsive beat and piano. It was inspired by a feel of a song he'd been hearing on the pop radio station he'd been listening to—a Khalid song, if he remembered right.

"Oh, that's dope, Jake." Kate bobbed up and down, adding flourishes to the piano part. She began to sing a harmony along with Jake. "I miss you more . . . I miss you more . . ."

Pretty soon they had finished the chorus lyrics, and then they dove into the verse melody and lyrics. By 3:00 p.m., they had a finished song that both of them were dancing around the room about. Throughout the process, Kate was going through a litany of artists to whom they could pitch the song—first their name and then identifying their label and management. She was already strategizing how to get the song to the right people in order to get the song recorded by the artist. It was fascinating to watch. Kate was a beast. For his part, Jake was used to writing a song and sending it to his publisher to have them try and get the song cut. But Kate could connect the business dots better than anyone he had ever seen. No wonder she was so successful. Not only was she writing great songs, but by filling the well, she was also able to know where the key people were in the music business who could help get that particular song into the right hands.

Later that evening, Jake was having dinner with a buddy at Pinewood Social Club in downtown Nashville when his phone rang. The caller ID read "SIR KID."

"Jake, Daniel here," he said with that precise accent when Jake answered. "I hope Kate didn't beat you up too badly today. She said she enjoyed the session."

"Kate Boom lowered the 'boom' on me, Daniel." Jake laughed and walked past the bar of the restaurant. "Oh, she took me to task all right. Made me realize I gotta get off my butt and start relearning my business."

"Yes, she doesn't pull punches when she's quizzing you, but there's a method to her madness. Too many times we put blinders on in our business pursuits, and we don't see all the machinations happening around us—movements that would help us accomplish our task. But we have such tunnel vision we often can't see it."

"Yeah, that, and add in a little laziness on my part," Jake said. "It's all stuff I've needed to hear. I've been on cruise control too long."

"Jake, you're no exception," Daniel said over loud background music. "Everyone falls prey to getting in a rut. Part of the ethos at The Row is we all have each other's backs, and we all help each other. It keeps all the writers from just punching the clock, so to speak."

"Well, I gotta say, Daniel, this week and The Method, at least so far, has been great for me." Jake was now outside the restaurant where it was quiet. "The creative collaboration session with Brit and Misha was amazing. We got a great song, but just the way they . . . I mean, the way *we* collaborated. It was unlike anything I'd ever done before. No one had an agenda other than writing the best song, producing the best work possible."

"Right," Daniel agreed.

"And then today with Kate. Her knowledge of the business and her insight. Damn, it was inspiring. It makes me realize I'm a lot more capable of getting things done than I'd thought. I've just been handing the work off and crossing my fingers."

"We're all guilty of doing the same thing. Humans everywhere, we tend to take the path of least resistance. We're all 'default' creatures. Do the easiest thing and move along. I'm afraid it's part of the human condition."

"Daniel, don't get all philosophical on me," Jake laughed and turned up the southern twang in his voice. "I'm just a simple musician!"

"You laugh, Jake," he said over the thump of loud dance music, "but you're a genius."

"Ah well, you're too kind, Daniel." Jake liked the sound of "genius."

"Do me a favor, Jake. Next week we're going to set you up with Dara Delaney and Shane Sawyer. You heard of them?"

"Of course." Shane was a Music Row legend, and Dara had all those amazing cuts with Miranda Lambert. Jake had been a fan of Shane's writing for years and had only recently learned about Dara. "I didn't know they were with The Row."

"Oh yes. For about a year it was big news in Nashville, Jake. Now that you've been schooled by Kate Boom, you're going to know these kinds of things in the future, correct?" Daniel laughed a bit, and the music in the background got quieter for a moment, then cranked up again. "I want you to start trying to apply The Method to all parts of your life. Reach out, work with people, collaborate in life."

"Well, sure," said Jake. "I get it. I'm already seeing how I've been in a creative rut. And it's been by my own hand. Now, just with the sessions with Brit and then Kate, I'm seeing how to break out of that. And I'm doing it. Been feeling more inspired in this week than I have in ages."

"Yes, I love that! Make it your goal to know what's going on around you, as well." His voice was barely audible over the music. "Fill the well."

"I totally get what you're saying, Daniel." Jake found himself feeling more than a little bit inspired by this conversation. "Where are you by the way? It's crazy loud."

"Oh yeah, the noise. I flew over to see David Guetta opening his residency in Ibiza. He's an old friend. It's 3:00 a.m. and madness over here!"

"Wait, you're in Ibiza right now? In the Mediterranean?" Jake shook his head. "I thought you were upstairs all day when I was working with Kate."

"Well, I was for a bit, but then I hopped on our little corporate jet, and here I am." He was shouting over the music now. "I'd better go, or Mr. Guetta will think I'm ignoring him."

"Ha, yeah, you better pay attention!" Jake walked back into Pinewood Social realizing how amazing these people were and how much his life and expectations had changed already.

"Oh, Jake, one last thing. How's that song coming along? The greatest song ever?" Daniel sounded focused again over the background noise. "Starting to hear the melody for it yet?"

"Uh, yeah." Jake couldn't be sure if he were serious or not. "I got a notion or two, and I'll keep you posted."

Daniel was back to shouting over the music. "Ah yes, okay, Jake. I can't wait to hear it. Cheers!"

And with that, Sir Daniel hung up, and the "genius" Jake Stark walked back into the gleaming Friday night establishment with more than just the hint of pep in his step.

RULES FOR FILLING THE WELL

1. Embrace the successes of your competition. Learn from them and be inspired by what they are doing right. Remember, you can't compete if you don't know what you're competing against.

2. We are all the product of our experiences, and when we create, we draw upon those experiences. Therefore, it's incumbent upon us that we continue filling the well of experience and inspiration.

3. Stay on top of the business of your business. Utilize and make the most of trade journals, charts, podcasts, and business news to be able to connect the dots on how to get work done. When you know what is happening in your business, you can more clearly see and know how to navigate your industry and be successful.

4. You can't give what you don't have. If you don't keep filling the well, it will run dry, just like an overdrawn bank account. Avoid creative bankruptcy by seeking out inspiration.

5. The more you learn, the bigger the return.

VERSE *(vers) n.* part of a song that contains the lyrical narrative or theme ‖ place in a song where the lyrics change ‖ where the listener is first introduced to the melody of the song.

Chapter 5

GREAT DAY

Checking his email Saturday morning, Jake saw one from Misha. Just as Daniel had suggested the night before, his next write with The Row would be the following Wednesday with Dara Delaney out at her place on Old Hickory Lake.

Well, the hits keep coming! Jake thought. *Brit Kanuka, Kate Boom, and now Dara Delaney? Does Daniel Smith-Daniels know something about me that I don't?* Brit and Kate were hot, young writers, but Dara . . . Well, she was the most in-demand writer in Nashville.

Misha also mentioned Jake had a write next Friday with Shane Sawyer. Shane was a Nashville legend. He'd written hits—massive ones—for George Strait, Reba McIntire, and Garth Brooks. He'd also started his own music publishing company, had signed many other songwriters, and had hits with them, as well. Jake recalled he'd sold the publishing company for some major dollars. He'd thought Shane had retired, but apparently not. Shane was also an accomplished pilot, and after he sold his publishing company, everyone figured he'd spend his time flying to tropical destinations around the world. Why not, right?

Clearly, though, Shane was back at it and now writing at The Row. Jake still couldn't get over the talent that Daniel had assembled in such a short time.

Before those writes, though, Jake had his writing appointment with Brie. On Tuesday morning around 11:00 a.m., Brie showed up at Jake's studio in Berry Hill. It was a little place he shared with a couple other writers. They called the studio The Goldmine—tongue-firmly-planted-in-cheek. Berry Hill was just a stone's throw from Music Row. It's where some of Nashville's best studios were located, including Blackbird and Sound Emporium.

"Good morning, Brie," said Jake as he opened the door. "Just in time for some fresh coffee."

"Yay!" Brie exclaimed, just a little bit overenthusiastic. "It's gonna be a great day!"

They jumped right into it, and Jake's initial hesitation about writing with an unknown, unsigned songwriter quickly melted away. Brie was a natural, with a gift for hooky melodies and a quick wit for lyrics. And to think he wouldn't have reached out to her if he hadn't been practicing contrary action. In the past, he would never have "wasted his time" working with an unknown with no track record, but here he was now, writing with Brie and having a blast.

She had an absurdly simple idea for a song called "Outta This World." It was like a nursery rhyme. Jake really let Brie guide the direction and offered his sage advice and ideas where needed. He couldn't help but think about what he'd learned from the session with Brit and Misha a week ago. He didn't try to run the session as he would've in the past; instead, he just let it go where it wanted. They both checked out some different songs that were currently on the charts to get some ideas for beats for the track Jake was building.

I'm filling that well, Kate, Jake thought.

Brie wrote using a ukulele, which was perfect for the breezy reggae feel of the song. The melody they had for the track was amazing, but there was something still lacking in the lyrics they were working on. The verse described the perfect morning:

You're the kiss that wakes me up
You're the coffee in my cup
Ray Charles on the radio
Heartbeats in stereo
Give me good, good morning...

You're outta this world . . .

The payoff chorus lyric—"You're outta this world"—just didn't fit. It felt disjointed. Jake was flipping it back and forth in his head.

Then he thought about what Brie said when she showed up at the door of the studio this morning.

"Brie, you know," Jake said, strumming the guitar, "I think we can beat the chorus lyric."

"Oh, I'm so glad you said something. I do too," said Brie. "It just doesn't feel right, does it?"

"How about . . ." Jake sang the verse and pre-chorus and then his chorus lyric. "*Give me good, good morning . . . Make a great, great day.*" It was deceptively straightforward, stupid even, but it worked. It was the kind of lyric that Jake would never use in a country song-writing session, but here, in this setting, it just worked perfectly.

"Oh, that's it!" Brie stood up and danced around, waving the ukulele. "Make a great, great day."

They worked straight through lunch, and by 1:30 p.m. that day, they had written the second verse and bridge and had even done a rough demo. It all happened fast.

"Jake, thank you so much. This was a blast." Brie said as she packed up her laptop and ukulele. "I love our song."

"You know, it's really good. Like 'Don't Worry, Be Happy' good."

"Right?" Brie laughed and put on her backpack. "Oh, I'm gonna play it for my songwriting class next week. Our teacher told us we have a special guest who's gonna come and listen to our songs."

"Cool. Well, let me know what this special guest thinks of our little ditty." Jake stood up and walked Brie out of the studio and to the front door.

"Okay. Thanks again, Jake," Brie said as she walked out the front door to her beat-up old Prius. "I will keep you posted!"

"The pleasure was mine, Brie. Bye-bye!" Jake waved and went back into the studio.

As he sat down at his desk, he found himself humming the simple little song they had just written. It really was good.

He reflected on the past week and a half or so. Something was definitely starting to happen with him—and not just with his songwriting. The meeting with Sir Daniel, the creative collaboration session with Brit and Misha, and the filling the well session with Kate, they had all had an impact on him—but deeper than just work and songwriting. It was hard to explain.

Jake had noticed it this past weekend when he was spending time with Sarah and Mac. He was present and engaged. Spending time on Sunday with family friends, Jake had decided to listen more to what people were saying, *really* listen, instead of thinking of what he would say in response. Just listening. And where he wanted to correct someone or out-do someone, he bit his tongue, practicing a little contrary action, collaborating in just a friendly conversation. He found that he was using what he'd learned in The Method sessions in his life. When a song came on the radio, he didn't dismiss it because it had been a band that didn't use one of his songs. Instead, he listened to what was great about the song, what he could learn from it.

I'm definitely drinking the Kool-Aid, but The Method stuff is working, thought Jake as he worked on the track he and Brie had just written, and the longer he spent fleshing out the track, the more he realized there was something really special about their little song.

Chapter 6

PRACTICE THREE: *LEAVING YOUR COMFORT ZONE*

Wednesday morning started as usual with the delicate strains of Harry Nilsson's "Everybody's Talkin'," and after a quick breakfast and coffee at Frothy Monkey on Twelfth Avenue South, Jake was off to write with Dara Delaney.

Now, Dara had a story. Taking a cue from his write with Kate last Friday and filling the well, as instructed, Jake had done a bit of due diligence on Dara on Sunday afternoon.

She'd grown up in Montana on her parents' ranch, where she learned to be an expert horse rider and was actually on the professional rodeo circuit after she'd finished college in Missoula. She'd also started playing guitar and writing songs along the way. The legendary John Prine had seen her play when she opened for him at the Mangy Moose in Jackson Hole, Wyoming, and he fell in love with her. He became her champion, and soon Dara was signed to a small Americana music label and moved to Nashville—as was the usual trajectory. At the same time, Dara began writing for other artists: everyone from Thomas Rhett and Maren Morris to Ariana Grande. She was a triple threat: songwriter, performer . . . and horseback rider.

As Jake was driving to Old Hickory Lake, which was northeast of downtown Nashville, he got a text from an unknown Montana number. Jake guessed it must be from his cowriter.

> Hey, honey, it's Dara. When you get to the house just park and walk around back to the boathouse. See you soon!

Jake texted back when he got to a red light.

> Copy!

He hit send as the light turned green.

Jake had been listening to the pop radio station on the drive up; in fact, that's what he'd been listening to pretty much all the time. Since he'd met with Brice last week, he'd gotten up to speed on some of the current hot artists inhabiting the charts, and the one on the radio right now sounded like Post Malone. Really cool production—not so much the song, but the way the track was put together made it feel fresh and current. Jake realized that in order to be competitive, he needed to collaborate with someone who could bring that kind of sound to his tracks. He decided to ask Misha if The Row had any up-and-coming producers he could work with, maybe form a production team.

Within fifteen minutes, exactly as Waze had predicted, Jake was out in front of Dara's lake house. It was a sprawling, '70s-style ranch house framed by huge oak trees and the vast, brown Old Hickory Lake behind it. Jake parked his car in the drive and grabbed his guitar and backpack. As he walked closer, he could see that while the house looked to have been built quite a while ago, it had clearly been vastly renovated. Peering through the windows as he walked up the drive, Jake could tell that it was stunning inside. He was about to knock on the front door when he remembered Dara had told him to go around the back to the boathouse.

Jake veered right off the driveway and onto a pea gravel path that appeared to go around the right side of the ranch house. As he walked through the trees on the path, he took in the gorgeous morning, which was shaping into a brilliant spring day. The temperature was warm but not overbearing, and the sky was a clear cobalt blue.

When Jake rounded the corner of the back of the house, he was blown away by the beauty of the backyard and lake beyond. By the looks of it, Dara had enlisted the help of some very talented landscapers to design an amazing space. A sprawling pool surrounded by rock outcroppings and flower beds anchored the center of the yard, while various hardscape sitting areas—one with a fire pit surrounded by a mini amphitheater—were strategically placed around the lush green yard. It was magical.

And oh yeah, there was a ping-pong table too.

Jake followed the path to the center of the yard where it split into three different directions. One path went to the pool, one to the back of the house, and one path—the one Jake chose—sloped down the yard toward the lake and the gorgeous boathouse.

"Okay, that's not a boathouse," Jake said under his breath. "That's a boat mansion."

The boat *mansion* was like a ranch house on steroids, with a massive glass-and-steel cube rising up from the back of the building. He tried to figure out how much this whole spread must have cost, and at the same time, how many hit songs it must have taken. He stopped on the walk to take a picture of the scene when—

"Boo!" came a loud voice with a midwestern twang from behind. Jake literally jumped into the air.

"Whoa!" He turned around to see who had snuck up on him. At first, he saw no one, and then he lowered his gaze.

"Well, howdy, partner," said a smiling and exuberant Dara Delaney, who couldn't have been more than five feet tall. And while Jake had done his due diligence before the write looking at Wikipedia and photos of Dara, who was usually dressed in jeans and cowboy attire, it still hadn't prepared him to find her right in front of him, wearing a floral cover up over a bikini and holding a tray of drinks with little umbrella straws in them.

"Whoa, hey, Dara. Jesus," he said, trying to get his bearings. "You scared the—"

"Horse manure out of you?" Dara laughed and scooted around Jake on the sidewalk down to the boathouse.

"Uh, yeah, well, I'm Jake . . . Jake Stark," he managed as he watched Dara head to the boathouse.

"Son, I know who you are," she called over her shoulder. "Follow me. Did you bring some swim trunks?"

"Ha, uh . . . no. I didn't think to pack them," Jake chuckled as he walked. Of course he didn't bring swim trunks.

"Oh, well, I sent you an email late last night that if the weather was nice—and it is, Jake, it's effin' beautiful—well, we'd take the float boat out. No worries, though. We got something lying around for you in the boat house, I reckon."

Hmm. Why do I have a bad feeling about this?

Jake caught up with Dara as she got to the side door of the boathouse and helped her with the door as she tried to negotiate the doorway without knocking over her tray of drinks. Now while the outside of the boathouse—and the yard, for that matter—were immaculate, the huge open den they walked into was a mess—like, a pigsty kind of mess.

"Good lord, look at this place!" Dara yelled as she stepped over some boots and looked around the open expanse of the boathouse's great room. It looked like a party, a knock-down-drag-out kind of party, had happened here. "Dan! Tom! Come on, guys. Rise and shine!"

Dara looked back at Jake and shook her head.

"Pardon the mess, Jake. We had a number-one celebration last night." Dara put her hand on top of her head. "We finished early, and I thought everything had been cleaned up, but clearly Dan and Tom kept the party going once they got back here." She turned back toward the room. "Yo, Tom, Dan, wakey wakey."

"What's the number one song?" Jake asked as he picked up a little wastebasket next to a sofa and started putting empty beer bottles and Taco Bell bags into it.

"Well, it was for two number ones I wrote with The Walker Brothers for Thomas Rhett: 'Come on Back' and 'Flip.'" Dara shook her head. "That's right, *Walker brothers*, it's time to write. Now! Vámanos!"

Just then, up on the landing, coming out of what must have been two different bedrooms, were Dan and Tom Walker, both wearing Hawaiian-print shirts and swim trunks.

"Aw yeah, let's do this," said Tom Walker, looking a little punch-drunk and hoisting his arms over his head touchdown-style.

"Just get me some aspirin and Gatorade, and I'll be good to go," said a not-as-animated Dan Walker.

Jake knew the Walker Brothers; in fact, he'd written with them more than a few times, but it had been a while since he'd seen them. Tom and Dan had been around Nashville for years. Starting in the early 2000s, the boys were a recording act on Sony Records and made a respectable run for a few albums. They had toured a lot when Big and Rich were everywhere, and they had kind of ridden the country-rock circus sideshow trend until the hits quit coming. Who could have known that their biggest success would come as writers for other artists? Well, Jake could've, of course, since his career had followed the same story arc.

Dan and Tom made their way down the stairs to the floor level, where Jake and Dara were cleaning up the party mess.

"Aw, hell." Dan looked around the room. "I know I was a little bit overserved, but jeesh this is ugly."

"You think, boys?" Dara sounded mad, but then she winked at Jake. "I don't want to even think of the characters you had here in my nice new boathouse."

"You don't even want to know, Dara." Tom Walker used his fingers to open his eyes wider. "Ugly, just ugly. Probably oughta have a hazmat team doing this."

"Well, I've made a little pick-me-up to jump-start your engines this morning." Dara walked over to her tray of umbrella-laden cocktails. The drinks looked frosty and dark green.

"Uh, no, I can't ever have any alcohol again . . . ever," Dan said and made a cross with his index fingers and pointed it in the direction of the drinks.

"Oh, ha!" Dara laughed. "This ain't firewater, honey. It's my own green juice recipe: kale, carrots, blueberries, turmeric, collagen protein, MCT oil, ginger . . . I could go on, but trust me, this will make you feel fit as a fiddle in no time. Provided you can get it down. Got one for you too, Jake."

Jake grabbed a drink off the round tray, which he could now see was actually an old tambourine.

"Wow, this is tasty," Jake said after he took a sip. "Man, it's got a kick."

"Momma likes her ginger," Dara said and stepped over a pair of boots on her way over to Dan and Tom at the foot of the stairs. "That'll open up your sinuses real good."

After the green juices and some chitchat while doing a bit more cleaning up in the boathouse, the discussion turned to the day's write. The four of them walked outside by the docked pontoon boat.

"Jake, what we're gonna learn today is the third practice in The Method," Dara said as she stepped off the dock and onto the boat. She had her guitar in one hand and her laptop backpack in the other. "You gotta leave your comfort zone, son. Today we're gonna leave that sucker on dry land."

"Oh, I got ya, Dara," Jake told her. "I haven't been on a boat since I don't remember when. And I certainly haven't tried to write on one, definitely never on a party barge like this!"

"Party barge," Dan Walker shouted as he and his brother stepped onto the boat as well. "Is that our song title?"

Tom Walker started mouthing the sound of a banjo as he stepped onto the boat.

"We're living large on the party barge," Dan sang over Tom's mouth banjo.

"Ha, I like it!" Dara said as she sat down in the captain's chair. "Now, Jake, captain's rules—and I'm the captain—state that everyone has to wear a bathing suit of some kind before they can step onto this fine watercraft. If you didn't bring any skivvies, I've got some hanging in the head over there."

Dara pointed to a door to the left of the sliding glass door they had walked out of. Painted on the door were the words "Little Sailors."

"Well, let me see what you got in there." Jake looked a little sideways at Dara. Why did he feel like he was being set up?

"I'm sure you can find something that'll fit ya," Dara said and then turned to Tom and Dan. "Can one of you boys ice down the drinks in the Yeti? There's an ice maker in the utility room over yonder."

"Sure thing, Dara," Tom said and hopped up from a couch on the pontoon boat. "We're gonna need some ice-colds while we're out there."

While they got prepared for the boat trip to write . . . whatever it was, Jake walked tentatively over to the "Little Sailors" room. When he turned on the lights, he was surprised by how spacious and nice the half bath was. It was all marble and silver fixtures. The white walls were lined with platinum albums and awards from BMI and others, while the floors were terrazzo with abstract designs. Right in front of the toilet, written in mosaic on the terrazzo floor, were the words "It all starts with a song." It was a beautiful room as far as bathrooms go, but Jake didn't see any bathing suits. He opened the cabinet doors under the sink but found nothing. He stuck his head outside.

"Yo, Dara, I see a lot of platinum in here, but no bathing suits."

"Oh, Jake, I know there's one. It's on the towel rack next to the commode," Dara said, looking up from the ice chest, and Jake could have sworn he heard a bit of a giggle in her voice.

"Nope, I'm looking, and I don't see—" Jake was scanning the three towel racks when he saw what looked like a white silk glove lying over the towels. No wonder he hadn't noticed it before; it was almost invisible against the towels. "Wait a second..."

Jake walked closer to the towel rack, and he could swear he heard one of the Walker brothers howl in the distance, and as he got closer, he could see why. What looked like a white silk glove, which is an odd enough thing to be hanging in a Tennessee boathouse bathroom, was actually a bathing suit. Jake reached out toward it.

"Uh, ha ha, no way." Jake said as he used his pinkie to hook the weenie bikini off the towel rack. This wasn't a Speedo brief. No, Speedo briefs were board shorts compared to this. This was something that might have been worn by Channing Tatum in *Magic Mike*. This was a piece of Lycra dental floss. Jake laughed and was about to shout out the open door that there was no way in hell he was going to don this suit, if it could even be called that. But then he thought about everything that had happened the past couple of weeks—the improbability of it. The Method, Daniel Smith-Daniels, Brit, Kate, the "Great Day" song with Brie that he couldn't get out of his head... everything.

Aw, to hell with it, Jake thought as he closed the door. *You want some contrary action? Well, contrary action coming right up!*

Jake moved over in front of the sink and took a look at himself in the bathroom mirror. He swung the silky swimsuit on his pinky next to his head.

So this is what it's come to. Jake smiled, then he sat down on the toilet and took off his beat-up Chucks and skinny jeans. He put on the skimpy white swimsuit and went back to the mirror.

"Oh. My. God," he said out loud as he took in the horror of his forty-five-year-old, once-athletic-but-not-so-much-now frame. Waist up, it was normal Jake Stark, ball cap on, wearing an old Heart concert T-shirt, but below the waist, it was a scary night in Ibiza or, more likely, Myrtle Beach. What made the picture worse was that his T-shirt hung so low, it just looked like it was the only thing he was wearing.

If People Magazine *could see me now.*

Shaking his head, Jake pulled on his sneakers then rolled up his jeans and socks and put them under the sink. He opened the door and stepped outside.

"Behold the glory," Jake said as he walked out onto the dock. "And this is a phone-camera-free zone."

"Ha, bravo, son! Bravo!" Dara was standing in the captain's chair of the pontoon boat, clapping loudly.

Dan burst into a fit of laughter so all-consuming that he couldn't catch his breath.

"Damnit," Tom Walker shook his head, laughing too. "Other than those pasty white legs, you look better than I did."

"Oh, so this is some kind of initiation?" Jake was laughing now as he stepped onto the boat. He started to narrate the scene. "He felt obscene in his T-shirt, sockless Chuck Taylors, and . . . and . . ."

"Th-th-th-th-thong!" both Walker brothers sang out in unison. Jake was pretty confident this image wasn't what Sisqó had in mind when he'd recorded "Thong Song."

"Aw, man, you're right. This *is* a freaking thong." Jake was now standing in the center of the boat next to Dara. "Sorry, Dara, no one needs to see me like this. Look away!"

"It can't be unseen," Dan hooted.

"Jake, don't be so hard on yourself. You look better than most," Dara called to him as she started the engine. Tom and Dan were casting off the lines from the dock. "It's fun and stupid, and we all go through it at The Row . . . Well, the guys anyway. I'd never wear something like that." Dara snorted. "The boat happens to be my favorite way to illustrate leaving your comfort zone. But there's a serious part too, and it's this: when you uproot yourself from what you know, from your familiar surroundings, when you're off balance, figuratively and"—Dara hit the throttle, and the pontoon boat jumped forward, making Jake catch himself to avoid falling— "literally," Dara laughed, "well, that's when you come up with stuff that's really inspired."

"Well, this," Jake pointed to the bathing suit, "is going to inspire something."

"Nausea?" Dan blurted out, still laughing as he and Tom plopped down into captain's chairs. Dan leaned forward and started fooling with his phone and the boat's stereo.

"For real, Jake, you look good in that suit." Tom chuckled, and Jake remembered that Tom was the jokester of the two brothers. "Dara's right, though. When all of life is flying around you, with everything in flux, that's when you can come up with amazing ideas. You're forced to!"

"Tom, weren't you wearing that same suit when we wrote 'Flip'?" Dara looked back at Tom and then she opened up the pontoon boat's throttle, sending the craft speeding surprisingly fast along the smooth surface of Old Hickory Lake.

"Wow, yes. Was it a year ago that I was in that sexy suit?" Tom put his hand to the top of his head. "Crazy all the stuff that's happened since coming to The Row."

"Please, Dara, tell me this suit gets washed," Jake said and then the music poured out of the boat's speakers.

"Oh yeah, baby!" Dan stood up in the speeding pontoon boat and started dancing.

And of course, blaring from the boat speakers was Sisqó's "Thong Song."

The four of them laughed and sang along with the playlist for the next ten or so minutes until Dara began to slow the boat. Jake looked out and realized he was in a part of the lake he had never seen. It was stunning.

"Whoa, where are we?" He looked around, trying to get his bearings.

They were in a small, half-moon-shaped lagoon with rock walls reaching straight up from the shoreline, as though a giant ice cream scoop had taken a chunk out of the earth. The walls—they looked like granite—went up some thirty feet to trees that lined the rim. There were no houses, just the four of them on the pontoon boat, floating on the water's glass-smooth surface. Dan or Tom, one of them, turned off the stereo as Dara cut the engine. In an instant, there was simple and pure silence. First, only silence. Then Dan spoke.

"Well, this doesn't suck," Dan deadpanned and reached into the Yeti cooler.

"Dan, damnit, shut the hell up." Dara looked around. "Don't spoil this unspoiled moment. I tell you this place is special—my favorite spot on all of the lake."

It got quiet again, save for Tom walking up to the front of the boat where the guitar cases were secured. He pulled his beat-up Martin D-12 from its case and sat down on the cushioned couch at the bow of the boat. He fidgeted around with a few chords and feels and then settled in on a gorgeous minor-key, finger-picked chord progression. Immediately, Dara started humming along a melody. It went low to high, an octave's leap right at the top, and it suited Tom's guitar part perfectly. Jake looked out over the lagoon and began to sing some words over Dara's melody.

"Still waters, oh you're running deep . . . Filling up this empty heart . . . and washing over me," Jake sang at the top of his range in an almost falsetto.

"Still waters," Dan chimed in with his tenor voice, and he sounded amazing. "Pull this lover down . . . Wrap me in your silence, and never let me drown."

"Whooo-wee!" Dara exclaimed, "Holy shit, y'all, keep that going. It's fire!"

It *was* fire. The melody and feel of the song was instantly amazing, like Adele's "Someone Like You" crossed with Ed Sheeran's "Thinking Out Loud." For the next two hours, they burned through the verse, chorus, and bridge with all the lyrics and a full arrangement—all of it finished by 1:30 p.m. Done.

It went by in a creative flash. Jake had forgotten they were on a boat on Old Hickory Lake. And he'd certainly forgotten he was wearing what amounted to a piece of string.

Finally, Dara recorded a run-through of the entire song—a "work tape" as it was called—on her phone's voice memo app.

"Y'all," Dara looked around, wide-eyed, at Jake, Tom, and Dan, as if they had all just discovered a buried treasure. "Y'all, holy shit. This song is amazing."

"Like next-level, Grammy-award-winning shit," Tom said, setting his guitar down after two hours of playing. "Great work, you guys."

"Dude, it was that guitar part," Jake said and suddenly realized that for two hours, he had forgotten he was wearing a silken thong swimsuit. "And damn, Dara, that chorus melody. Insane!"

"No, it was the suit, Jake," Tom giggled. "I had to play something beautiful to counteract the horror of your getup."

"Dara, send that work tape to all of us so we don't lose that sonic gold!" Dan reached into the Yeti and tossed a beer to Tom.

"Oh, hell yes," Tom smiled and shook his head. "It's beer-thirty!" He popped the top on the beer, took a swig, sat it down, and did a backflip over the side of the boat.

"Jake, I got something for you," Dara said as she reached into a dry bag at the back of the boat. "It's here somewhere . . . Ah, voilà!"

Dara had reached her arm all the way into the dry bag and then pulled it out to reveal a proper pair of board shorts. She threw them at Jake.

"Now, for God's sake, put that on over the thong, son!"

"Whoa, wait." Jake caught the suit as it flew at him from the back of the pontoon boat. He held the swimsuit in front of him. "You dog. You had these the whole time?"

"Guilty as charged, your honor." Dara put her hand to her chest. "But it's my favorite way to get folks out of their comfort zones."

"Uh, I'll say. A bit extreme, but hey," Jake stood on one leg, wobbling a little as he pulled the swim trunks on, "we got a rad song."

"Yeah, we did." Dan's voice came up quickly behind Jake. "It's gonna make a splash!"

And then suddenly, Jake felt the push of Dan's hands on his back, and he launched over the side of the boat, swim trunks still only halfway up his legs.

"You son of a—" Jake shouted as his body splashed into the water, and whatever he was going to say was silenced by the cool, clear water of Old Hickory Lake.

RULES FOR LEAVING YOUR COMFORT ZONE

1. When life is in flux, when we are off balance, that's often when we are the most creative. In fact, we flourish when exposed to randomness, disorder, and stressors.

2. When we push into new creative zones outside our comfort zone, we build our self-confidence.

3. When we leave our comfort zone, we enter our growth zones where we realize our aspirations, set new goals, and find purpose.

4. When we leave our safe places, we're forced to come up with new ideas and strategies for completing our creative tasks.

5. Opportunities and ideas lie outside our comfort zone. We have to step outside our comfort zone in order to find them.

CHORUS *(kor-es)* *n.* contains the primary lyrical and melodic themes that will be repeated throughout the song ‖ conveys the main idea, and often contains the title of the song, as well ‖ the song's hook, the place that the listener should remember.

Chapter 7

PRACTICE FOUR: *CHANGE YOUR ATTITUDE*

Jake hopped into the old Rover on Friday and punched Shane Sawyer's address into the Waze app on his phone. It was an address he didn't recognize. When the directions popped up, Jake did a double take and checked the email from Misha to make sure it was correct: 1533 Flight Boulevard, Nashville, Tennessee. Jake read it again and checked the app. Yep, it was correct. Apparently Shane's studio was out at Nashville International Airport. An odd place to have a studio, not to mention a pain in the butt to get to.

Oh well. When you're Shane Sawyer, I guess you can have your studio anywhere you please. Bet he wants to show me his airplane.

Twenty minutes later, Jake arrived at the destination. It wasn't a studio address but rather a private aviation company called Billion Air. Jake parked his old truck between a new Bentley and a Mercedes G-Wagon.

"We're a little out of our league here," Jake said, patting the dashboard of the old Rover. "Don't get jealous. You're still my number one."

He grabbed his backpack and guitar from the back seat and headed into a glass two-story building flanked by private jets on the hot tarmac.

Okay, this is an odd place for a write, but whatever.

Jake walked through the front doors of the building and approached the young man behind the lobby desk.

"Mr. Stark," said the man. "Shane will be right out. He's in the restroom."

Before Jake could say anything, the men's room door opened, and none other than Nashville songwriting legend Shane Sawyer stepped into the lobby.

"Toby, you don't need to advertise that I'm in the head." Shane's deep Sam-Elliot-esque baritone echoed through the space, then he turned his attention to Jake. "How ya doing? Been entirely too long, Jake."

"Shane, pleasure to see you again, man." Jake was genuinely pleased to see Shane. He figured it had been maybe fifteen years since they had last seen each other. Shane walked over, and they slapped hands together in a handshake.

"Think it was around 2005 at the *CMA Awards*. We both got awards that night, I recall." Not only did Shane sound like Sam Elliott, but he looked and dressed like him too. Jake noted his head-to-toe denim outfit.

"Oh, that's right." Jake couldn't help but chuckle. "That was a good night. Need more like that!"

"Right, brother?" said Shane as he waved bye to Toby and headed out the door to the airplanes sitting on the tarmac. He motioned for Jake to follow. "The folks over at The Row told you we gotta make a little trip today?"

"In the airplane?" Jake asked, pointing toward the tarmac. "Actually, Misha just said we had a write, no other details . . . but I'm easy, ha. Where we gonna go?" *What the . . .? As if the past week and a half couldn't get any odder.*

"Brother, we are going to Louisville to pick up a little beauty. Check this out," Shane said as he and Jake walked out of the air-conditioned lobby and onto the tarmac. He held his phone up to Jake. "That right there is Brownie, Jake. Eric Clapton's '56 Strat. Played 'Layla' with that git-fiddle."

"Holy crap!" Jake was blown away. Of course, he knew the guitar. It was legendary. "I thought it was in a museum somewhere."

"Nope, just a collector's place up in Kentucky. Some big bourbon producer up there," Shane said as they got to what must be his airplane. "'Bout to be in the Shane Sawyer Museum."

"Uh, nice 'little' plane you got here, Shane." Jake's voice dripped with sarcasm. The "little plane" at the end of a royal-blue runway carpet was a gorgeous Cessna Citation X. Cost? About $2-$3 million . . . used.

Since he'd been a kid, Jake had always been a bit of a plane buff. Interesting, since he had also always been uneasy with heights and confined spaces, but the Cessna Citation would work just fine. "We're gonna get to Kentucky quicklike."

Shane laughed, looking back over his shoulder at Jake. "Oh, son, we're not taking the X. We're taking her!"

Shane Sawyer cut a sharp angle off the plush-blue carpet leading to the Citation and pointed at another plane sitting, lonely and quivering, against the fence line of the Billion Air property. Despite the heat coming off the tarmac, the sight of the plane sent an instant cold shiver through Jake's body. The plane Shane was pointing at was a Cessna all right, but not a Citation X . . . not by a long shot.

"Aw, hell, Shane!" Jake couldn't help but let a little concern come out of his mouth. "Is that a—"

"Cessna 150, baby!" Shane put his arms up in the air touchdown-style. He was walking backwards now, looking at Jake. His face was beaming. "Circa 1962—the year yours truly popped into the world."

Now up until this point, Jake had been game for everything. He'd jumped into creative collaboration with Brit Kanuka, filled the well with Kate Boom, and hell, a few days ago he'd left his comfort zone and literally leapt headfirst into Old Hickory Lake while writing a song on a pontoon boat with Dara Delaney and her crazy friends, but now . . . he was being asked to go up in a Cessna 150, a tiny, ancient, single-prop plane. Sorry, fifty-four years wasn't that old for a human, but for a plane—a single-prop Cessna—it was ancient, like something the Wright brothers would have flown. Not to mention, just a few years ago, a Cessna 150 had collided midair with an Air Force F-16. The results had not been good.

"Wow." That was all he could muster. He really felt like he was about to have a panic attack. "That's gonna be cozy."

"We're gonna get to know each other really well, Jake," Shane said as he practically giggled. He opened the little door of the Cessna as it let out a rusty sounding creak. "She may look a little battered and bruised, but you won't find a better, more efficient flying machine. Don't you worry yourself a bit, Jake. It'll be painless."

Yeah, painless. Until we're crashing into the ground. Jake shook his head. *What could I possibly learn from going up in a deathtrap like this?*

"All right, Jake. Hand me your guitar and backpack, and I'll slide 'em behind us here and make sure to strap 'em down nice and tight in case we hit any turbulence." Shane stuck his head inside the cockpit. "Whoa! It's hot in here today, damn!"

"Oh boy," said Jake as the wave of heat escaping from the little Cessna hit him. He was about to say he wasn't going to fly with Shane, but then Daniel's words came back to him.

"Practice contrary action, Jake."

"Shane, my instincts are telling me to 'wave off,' but damn if I'm not gonna get in this jalopy and fly with you up to Kentucky."

"That's the spirit, Jake," said Shane as he rounded the aircraft and hopped in the pilot's door directly opposite Jake. "There's a 'method' to the madness."

"Aha, I see what you did there, Shane." Jake tried to laugh as he slid into the passenger seat. The hot vinyl burned his legs through his jeans. "Let's get this baby up in the air and cool things down. My core is rising!"

"Yessiree," said Shane in his perfect Sam Elliott voice. "Let's get this hunk of junk up in the air!"

Within fifteen minutes, Jake and Shane were flying over Music Row and downtown Nashville and banking east, then due north towards Louisville, Kentucky. Jake was wearing the same kind of pilot's headset as Shane, but even with the headphones, the sound of the prop engine was deafening. They had not spoken since wheels up, but then Shane motioned to his headset and spoke into its microphone.

"Jake, turn on your noise reduction here," said Shane over the roar of the cabin. He had his index finger on a small button on the right ear of the headphone. Jake fumbled on the side of his headphones till he found the button and pressed it. As if by magic, the noise of the engine, the wind, everything, completely disappeared.

"Whoa, that's amazing," said Jake as his voice broke the relative silence. Now Jake was used to noise cancelling headphones, but this was next-level stuff. "Shane, this is insane! I've never heard anything like this."

"Or not heard, as the case may be." Shane smirked as he consulted the control panel on the Cessna.

"Who makes these? They're incredible." Jake scanned Shane's set, looking for a logo. The headsets were sleek and modern looking, but no logo.

"Well, actually . . . I do, along with some very talented individuals. You are wearing a prototype we're working on for the aviation industry."

"These sound stunning." Jake was absolutely blown away. "If you made these for consumers as just headphones for music—"

"Oh, son, don't you worry." Shane grinned at Jake. "That's next. I'll keep you posted and see if you want to jump in on it."

"It would be huge! I mean bigger than Beats. Just incredible sound." So, this is some of what Shane had been up to since selling his company, taking that money and developing these. "Yeah, man, please let me know!"

"You got it, pal," said Shane as he fidgeted with what looked like a radio lower on the instrument panel.

A second later, a low keyboard pad—something that sounded like a Fender Rhodes piano but through a synthesizer—came playing through the headphones. Jake realized Shane had simply turned on some music, something soft and atmospheric.

"So, Jake, tell me how your whole experience has been since you met with Sir Daniel Smith-Daniels. That's a mouthful, huh?" Shane looked straight ahead.

Jake thought back over the past couple of weeks. "Well, I gotta say, it's been pretty amazing. I mean, you know, I met my buddy, Brice Smith."

"Hell, I love Brice. Great guy. Now he's on a roll." Shane glanced at Jake. "Hitsville for that guy right now. Did he bring you into The Row? Introduce you?"

"Oh yeah, we hooked up for dinner, and he just kind of told me what you guys are doing over there."

"Brice was my first contact with The Row, as well," Shane said as the ambient music swelled slightly in Jake's headphones—nothing he would have predicted denim-clad Shane Sawyer would listen to.

"Yeah, when he mentioned Daniel . . . I mean Sir Daniel—" Jake said.

"I know, crazy, that guy. Twenty-eight or twenty-nine years old, and he's knighted by the Queen?"

"And The Method . . . Honestly, I kind of rolled my eyes," Jake said, looking down at the lush forests and farmland beneath them. "But hey, the hits Brice is having—"

"Yeah, someone who never had much success at all," Shane chimed in.

"And Brit and Kate Boom," Jake said. "And look, I haven't been on fire exactly the past few years. I figured, 'Why not? I want whatever they're having.'"

"Oh, I hear you," Shane said as he fiddled with a control on the plane. "I was really gonna check out of songwriting after I sold my publishing, but then after, I met with Daniel. Reluctantly, at first."

"Yeah," Jake chimed in.

"Well, I saw how the practices of The Method would benefit all aspects of my life, not just writing songs." Shane looked over at Jake. "Where are you at right now? Who have you written with so far?"

"I've had sessions with Brit and Misha, Kate, Dara Delaney . . . " Jake counted on his fingers.

"Ha, Dara! She's a piece of work, huh?" Shane slapped his leg, laughing.

"Oh, she's crazy," Jake said.

"Crazy good at writing," Shane said. "She's a riot."

"Oh man, we wrote on her pontoon boat with her friends—"

"The Walker Brothers?" Shane raised an eyebrow as he pulled the plane a little higher.

"Yes," Jake laughed.

"Oh, those guys are nuts." Shane rolled his eyes. "Were they drinking moonshine?"

"Oh yeah. I didn't partake, but they certainly did."

"Did you get a song written?"

"Somehow, we did . . . And it's really good," Jake said. He thought about the write a couple days ago. Talk about leaving your comfort zone, writing out on a boat . . . with some crazy hillbillies. But really, though, that was nothing compared to this. Flying in an ancient Cessna—a single-prop Cessna at that. Jake could feel the plane rising as Shane pulled back on the yoke.

"Jake, see that gauge right there?" Shane said, tapping his finger on the glass of the round screen.

"Yep, and whatever it is, seems to be going up." Jake could see the gauge was at 8,500 . . . 8,600 and climbing.

"You are correct. It is going up," Shane said.

"Is that the altitude?" Jake made an educated guess.

"Winner, winner, chicken dinner," Shane said loudly through the headphones. "Altitude is defined as the height of an object in relation to sea level or the ground, but what I wanna talk about is this." Shane tapped on another gauge that showed an outline of a plane—*their* plane, presumably—floating against a half-blue, half-black background.

"It's cool looking, whatever it is." Jake thought he'd seen this before but had no idea what it was.

"That's the key, Jake," said the best Sam-Elliott-but-not-Sam-Elliott voice ever. "And it's the reason I wanted you to fly with me today. Now, Jake, you know what altitude is but that, that right there," Shane tapped the gauge again, "that right there is your attitude, Jake, and you gotta change your attitude!"

"Yessir, Coach," said Jake playfully.

"I'm serious, partner. Attitude is your plane's orientation to the earth's horizon. Or put another way, it's your angle of approach, especially when you're landing. Are you nose up or down? Are you yawing left or right?" When he said "left or right," he pushed the yoke to the left and depressed a foot pedal. The plane was suddenly on its left side, angling higher and higher. Jake slid on the plane's bench seat until he was next Shane.

"Okay, I get it," Jake said, looking at the gauge and trying to scoot back to his seat. "It helps you determine. It tells you what your angle is when you're coming in for a landing, tells you what your angle of approach to the airport is, right?"

On the attitude gauge, the outline of the plane was at a forty-five-degree angle to the horizon. Jake's body could feel every degree of it.

"Exactly, Jake, and I like to think of it in songwriting or problem-solving terms too." Shane pushed the yoke forward, and instantly the nose of the Cessna began pointing downward. "What's your angle of approach when you write a song?"

"Like, how do I start a song?" Jake noticed that the plane was slowly edging towards a nosedive. He also noticed his fingers were digging into his legs.

"Yeah, with the guitar?" Shane remained perfectly calm as the plane was diving. At least the plane had leveled out and was no longer sideways.

"I guess most of the time I start with just strumming the guitar and seeing what comes from that." Jake was starting to get uneasy, and he could feel the heat rising in the cabin. His heart was beginning to beat faster, as well.

"Yeah, me too, but sometimes my usual way of writing a song—my usual angle of approach, if you will—ain't working." Shane remained calm as can be.

"Like when you're banging your head and nothing's coming?" Jake said, trying not to let his unease come through in his voice.

"Exactly. That's when you gotta change your attitude, son." Shane pulled up suddenly on the yoke. Jake could feel his internal organs settle back into their normal place after their brief weightlessness.

"Whoa, there we go!" said Jake in a boisterous voice. "That is a feeling you don't experience every day. Jeesh!"

"Well, you know, Jake," Shane laughed, "I gotta make my point."

"Point made, Shane." Jake held his hands up in mock supplication.

"It's easy. Changing your attitude is all about changing your angle of approach to accomplish a task. What can you do differently to break a creative impasse, you know? And the benefit isn't just *writing* a song, but it's often writing a *better* song by approaching it differently."

"Like disrupting the norm?" Jake finally felt normal again as the plane flew smoothly over the green-blue hills of Kentucky.

"Exactly! You sound like someone from Silicon Valley now." Shane laughed and slapped his leg as the plane jostled a bit. "Like, you know, if I'm trying to come up with a song idea on guitar, even in a session, and it's not happening . . . Well, I don't just drive it into the ground. I change my attitude. Maybe start with a cool drum beat and see if that kick-starts an idea."

"Sometimes I'll just start writing out lyrics instead of starting with a guitar." Jake's thoughts were coming together as he started to get back to his body's normal equilibrium. The ambient, atmospheric music that was playing through the headphones helped his mood too.

"Exactly! Just switching up that angle of approach always yields good results, especially when you're doing something creative." Shane eased back on the throttle a bit. "You know, one of my favorite ways of writing a song is by reverse engineering a hit song or something that you just really love."

"What do you mean exactly?" Jake looked out over the Kentucky countryside. He could see a city skyline in the distance. It looked like they were starting to descend a bit.

"Well, take a hit song and break it apart," Shane said. "What are the elements that make it great?"

"You mean like the beat, the melody, the instrumentation, the production?" Jake asked.

"Right. Just start pulling apart the song until you get to the building blocks. You can do it for anything really—anything in business too," Shane said. "Like, that's what the team and I did developing these headphones. We hit roadblock after roadblock, but we just kept approaching the challenges from different angles, and we finally had our breakthroughs. Ask yourself: What are the essential elements of a great song? A great idea? A great product?"

"Oh, that's cool," Jake said. "I mean, I guess I've done that a bit in the past, but not overtly."

"Well, you got to know what you're competing against if you're gonna compete." Shane adjusted gauges and levers as he spoke. "Breaking it apart helps."

"Ah, you're quoting Kate Boom, filling that well." Jake remembered Kate's words from his session last week. Suddenly, the music swelled in his headphones.

"Guilty as charged! But it really is about using different attitudes to accomplish the task."

"Man, what is this music? It's really cool. Kinda weird, but cool." Jake adjusted his headphones, shifting the earpieces to hear the music better.

"Oh, that'd be Brian Eno. I think this album is called *Music for Airports*." Shane scratched his chin. "Kinda appropriate, seeing as we're in a plane and all."

"Shane Sawyer is listening to Brian Eno?" Jake was surprised. Brian Eno was a British musician, producer, and avant-garde thinker who had been around since the '70s. He'd made solo albums, but had also produced huge albums for U2 and Coldplay. Jake realized this must be Eno's ambient music series that he'd put out way back in the '80s—really just atmospheric sounds with no real discernible song structure.

"Man, I've been digging these ambient albums forever. It's the perfect flying and thinking music," Shane said. "But also, I chose this music because I wanted to bring up Oblique Strategies." Shane glanced over at Jake.

"Say what? O . . . bleek what?"

"It's a deck of attitudes, if you will." Shane stopped and then spoke into the microphone of the headphones, this time talking to the control tower of whatever airport they were coming into. Then, he came back to Jake. "Eno—back in the late '70s, I guess—developed this stack of cards, like playing cards, to promote creativity . . . to help break creative blocks. Anyhow, on every card is a suggestion for what to do to change your attitude about whatever it is you might be trying to accomplish. It encourages lateral thinking."

"Uh, like, what do you mean? What kind of suggestions?" Jake was genuinely intrigued. He had always been a fan of Eno's work but had never heard of Oblique Strategies.

"Oh, there's tons of them. Let's see," Shane put his fingers to his lips. "Oh, like, 'Remove ambiguities and amplify specifics,' 'Faced with a choice, do both,' 'Honor your mistakes,' 'Abandon your normal instrument,' or my favorite: 'Take a break.'"

"Ha, okay, I get it, I get it." Jake saw how some of the suggestions could help kick-start a song when you weren't getting anywhere.

"Exactly, Jake." Shane pulled back on the yoke. "Now, make sure your belt is nice and tight. I'm about to perform my own little Oblique Strategy. It's called, 'Turn it upside down,' or as I like to say, 'Hold on to your ass!' "

And with that, Shane began to do what Jake would've thought was so totally and utterly crazy and dangerous to do—like worst-case scenario—that Shane never would've attempted it. Shane was pulling totally back on the yoke. They were headed straight up and over. Shane was going to do a loop in the sky with this old Cessna 150.

"Hang onto your hat, Jake," Shane yelled. "One attitude adjustment coming up!"

"You're crazy," Jake yelled back, his hands gripping the seat, his knuckles white as they went upside down. "Oh, shiii . . .!"

Somehow, minutes later, they landed safely, and a waiting black SUV took them north of Louisville to an amazing horse farm estate. Turns out the owner of Clapton's Brownie, Buddy Whelan, was a real estate mogul, thoroughbred owner, and a songwriter himself. Jake also discovered that part of the deal of buying the guitar was that Shane—and now Jake, by default—had to write a song with Buddy.

The session went great, though. Whelan had an unbelievable studio he had built on his estate, with beautiful rare instruments and recording equipment. He wasn't half bad as a songwriter. Of course, with Shane and Jake's help, they came up with the makings of an amazing song. They did a quick demo of the track with just guitar and vocals, and Jake took a thumb drive back with him to fully produce the track.

The flight home was uneventful—as in, there were no aerial acrobatics. Even Shane seemed a little tapped out after the flight up to Louisville.

That night, back home at the dinner table with Sarah and Mac, Jake recounted the day's events. Mac thought it was cool and asked if he could go with Jake next time he went flying with Shane. Sarah, though, seemed upset, and Jake guessed correctly that it was the whole husband-in-an-aeronautical-stunt-show thing, among other concerns.

"It's just too dangerous, Jake," Sarah said. "I don't like hearing about that kind of stuff. You have too much to lose, and please don't get Mac excited about it either."

Jake's first instinct was to try and counter her concerns and say that it was fine and that she shouldn't worry so much, that she was overreacting. But then he thought of contrary action, and he also thought about changing his attitude. If he proceeded with the way he normally approached this kind of conversation with Sarah, he knew they wouldn't accomplish anything, and they would both end up being upset. Instead, he approached it differently.

"You know what? I don't disagree with you. Yes, it was crazy fun—"

"Jake—" Sarah began.

"*But* . . . but it was also just plain crazy to be in that fifty-plus-year-old plane doing that kind of stuff," he continued. "I really didn't have a choice. Once we were up in the air, Shane just went rogue and did what he was going to do. He was illustrating a point, but I think he went overboard a bit."

"You think?" Sarah looked Jake square in the eye. "No more flying with Shane, okay?"

"You have my word, babe." Jake put his arms around her. "No more flying with Shane Sawyer. Hopefully some more writing though. He's great."

"We can agree on that." Sarah finally smiled. "He's one of the best there is."

"*You're* one of the best there is," Jake said.

"Okay, I'll accept that," Sarah said, and hugged him. "Now go make sure your son takes a shower. He's filthy."

"Yes, ma'am," Jake said as he walked through the den to the hallway.

There just might be something to this "change your attitude" stuff after all . . .

RULES FOR CHANGING YOUR ATTITUDE

1. Attitude in aviation is your relationship to the earth's horizon, or more specifically, your angle of approach in landing. You can look at creative problem-solving in the same way.

2. We all have various tools we possess that can accomplish creative tasks. The challenge is to use them.

3. When the normal angle of approach to completing a creative task isn't working, we must change our attitude and approach our task differently.

4. Reverse engineering is a great creative tool to see how a song, an idea, or a successful business started originally. Break it down to its essential elements, and it will often kickstart a new idea.

5. There is no one way of doing something, only ways we haven't thought of yet. When we approach our tasks differently, we discover fresh ways to accomplish creative goals.

Chapter 8

EVERYBODY'S TALKIN'

The next day after a quick workout at the gym (five days in a row!), Jake was in his writer's room off Music Row bright and early. It was nice to not have a write that day, which meant that Jake could concentrate on making a full demo of the song he had written yesterday with Shane and Buddy Whelan. He still couldn't believe that Shane pushed the little Cessna plane that hard. Sarah was right; it was crazy. Still, though, he got a good song out of it. A Shane Sawyer song at that. Never mind that he had to fly into the open maw of the grim reaper in order to get it. Crazy that just having Shane's name on the song alone would ensure that people would listen to it with a different set of ears, as in, "It must be good if Shane Sawyer was a part of it."

Jake fired up the desktop computer and turned on the preamps and other recording equipment. Once it was all up and running, he searched his phone for the voice memo of the song they wrote up in Louisville. Ah, there it was: "Keep Running." Jake hit PLAY and sat back in his Aeron chair. He could hear the three of them joking around and then Shane started playing the opening chords on Brownie, Clapton's old guitar. Jake was singing the song, a rolling, "driving music" kind of song with finger-picked guitar.

The lyrics painted the picture of a race car driver who had not only lost his winning ways but also the love of his life. It was a melancholy song, but it felt great, and there was something that was super familiar about it. Try as he might, Jake couldn't put his finger on it. It wasn't that they were "stepping on something," as they said in Nashville, or using elements of someone else's song. No, it was just a feel, and it was driving Jake crazy. He closed his eyes and tried to summon which song it was reminding him of. Still, nothing.

After a few more minutes, Jake let it go and began to work on the track.

He started with recording the acoustic guitar, beginning to end. Then, when he was satisfied with the guitar part, he began building a drum track over the guitar using a sample library in a drum application. It was tedious work, but Jake loved it, piecing together the different parts of the recording. The drums, the bass, the acoustic guitar—when Jake played and recorded, well, there was a deep satisfaction he got when he finally hit PLAY, and suddenly there was a fully formed band playing, the song leaping out of the speakers.

The track was sounding good, really good. Jake felt that the finished song would have a definite crack at getting cut by a variety of artists. Shane Sawyer song or not, this track was a hit. But something was still missing. That certain "spice" that the track needed to stand out from the thousands of songs getting pitched just wasn't there. Jake played the track one more time and then decided to grab lunch at the Meat and Three diner down the block from his studio.

Now, if you don't know what Meat and Three is, then you haven't been to Nashville. In the old-school restaurants around Middle Tennessee, a feature on many menus is your choice of a meat—roasted chicken, beef, ribs, etc.—and your choice of three vegetables or sides. Today, at Dottie's on The Row, the meat of the day was stewed chicken, and that was exactly what Jake Stark would be having, along with lima beans, corn, and broccoli.

Jake walked to Dottie's humming "Keep Running," and even while he was there eating and saying hello to the occasional songwriter, he still had the song in his head.

What was the missing part?

"Well, that's a got-a-song-stuck-in-my-head look if I've ever seen one," said a familiar voice.

Jake looked up from his almost spotless plate—he had inhaled his lunch. Before him stood Chuck Lane. In the same outfit he always wore, what the locals called a Tennessee tuxedo—jean jacket, chambray shirt, and faded True Religion jeans—he looked like somebody from another life. That's because he was.

"Nothing changes if nothing changes." Those words Chuck had said when he gave Jake the news about his contract reverberated in his brain.

"Chuck," Jake said. "The myth, the legend. Take a seat."

"How you doing, Jake?" Chuck sat down in the chair opposite him.

"Man, Chuck," Jake felt ready to be about as honest as he had ever been. "I'm amazing. I've had the craziest, amazingest—if that's a word—uh, most fulfilling past couple of weeks."

"Oh yeah," said Chuck. "I heard Daniel Smith-Whatever-his-name-is was courting you over at Music Row. Does that have something to do with it?"

"Ha, well, yeah. Word travels fast on Music Row." Jake shrugged. "But I gotta say, they have an amazing group of writers over there, and there's just this vibe, this ethos I guess you'd call it, that is just inspiring."

"Hmm." Chuck raised an eyebrow.

"Seriously." Jake immediately reacted to the dubious look on Chuck's face. "There's a reason *Sir Kid*"—Jake made air quotes with his fingers—"is a billionaire. He just has a fresh and inspiring way of approaching things. It's cool, and you know me, Chuck, I'm the first person to say someone is full of crap."

"Oh, you're right about that." Chuck laughed. "Oh, I almost forgot. Brie Turner. You know her, right? You've worked with her?"

It took Jake a second.

"Brie? Belmont-student Brie?" Jake asked.

"One and the same." Chuck slapped his hand on the table.

"Yeah, she's the daughter of a friend I went to high school with. Wrote with her last week. How do you know her? Is she interning?" Jake was genuinely surprised.

"Well, her songwriting instructor at Belmont, Blake Darrow—"

"Blake? He's teaching now?" Jake was surprised. "We used to raise a little hell back in the day."

"Yeah, he's a character. Anyhow, he sent me some of her songs, and they're really good. I think I'm going to sign her to MegaMusic."

"Whoa, that's amazing," Jake said, genuinely happy for Brie but also just a little stung that the guy who dropped him from MegaMusic was talking about signing a new writer. He got over it quickly. "She's really good."

"Yeah, she is, and one of my favorite songs is the one you two wrote: 'Great Day.' I think that's a big ol' hit."

"That is a good one. Just silly enough to be massive." Jake threw down some cash to pay his bill and got up to walk out. Chuck followed.

"Well, you know, Jake," Chuck said to Jake before they went opposite ways on Sixteenth Avenue South. "I'm a big enough man to admit I might have made a mistake not re-upping your deal. If you're still a free agent—"

"Ha!" Jake laughed. "Thinking you put me out to pasture a little too soon, Chuck?"

"Now just hold on . . ." His voice trailed off. "But seriously, consider the offer still out there, if you're interested."

"All right, good to know." Jake patted Chuck's shoulder. "As you told me, Chuck, 'Nothing changes if nothing changes.' "

"Touché." Chuck grinned, they shook hands, and Jake began walking back to the studio.

Whoa, Chuck is signing Brie? What a world I live in that "Great Day" is considered an amazing song. Well, good for her. Good for me!

Back in the studio, Jake opened up his recording program and listened back to the Shane Sawyer song. It sounded great, but there was still that missing "thing."

Okay, Jake, let's use what Shane was trying to teach you during the aerial acrobatics. How do I change my attitude on this one? What's a different angle of approach for cracking the code on this song?

Jake moved the computer cursor back to the top and hit PLAY, only he didn't start it far back enough. As a result, the song started about three seconds in, on the turnaround chord. It was a D chord, and the second he heard it, he instantly knew what the missing element was, what song it was reminding him of.

It was "Everybody's Talkin'" by Nilsson, the song he woke up to every day.

"Holy crap!" Jake said out loud over the playback of the song. "If it was a snake, it woulda bitten me."

He instantly knew the way to break the creative gridlock of the song was to use a sample of the Nilsson song—actually take part of the Nilsson recording and massage it into "Still Running."

"One attitude change, coming up," Jake said out loud. "It was right there all along."

Jake found the Nilsson song in his computer's music library. He played it back over the speakers and listened to see if there was a snippet he could sample and loop for use in "Still Running." Ah, there it was, the main guitar figure of "Everybody's Talkin'" would be a perfect sample for his song, only it was in a different key. But that wouldn't be a problem. Jake recorded the roughly four-second sample of the Nilsson song, then he made a new track, dropped the sample in, and hit PLAYBACK.

"Ouch!" Jake said aloud as he heard the chord clashing against the different key of "Keep Running." "Okay, let's fix you."

Jake then opened up a pitch-change app and dropped the sample in. Checking with his acoustic guitar, he figured out he needed to lower the pitch of the Nilsson sample. He moved the cursor, hit RENDER, and then listened back to the song.

Suddenly what had been just another good but run-of-the-mill song was transformed. It was breathtaking. The sample of the old '70s song under his new song gave it a texture and vibe that sounded completely fresh and modern and . . . timeless.

"Houston, we have liftoff!" Jake said as he stood up and danced around the room.

He couldn't believe the key to the song was right under his nose all the time, but it wasn't until he opened up his mind to approaching the song differently—changing his attitude, as Shane put it—that he was able to make the song really work.

Okay, Sir Kid, your tricks really work, you young, rich, genius bastard. Jake laughed to himself. *Creative collaboration, filling the well, leaving my comfort zone—thong notwithstanding—and now changing my attitude...*

I get it. It works.

After a few minutes, once his excitement had died down and he had caught his breath from his impromptu dancing, Jake spent the next hour or so tweaking the track and cleaning up the sample a bit. He listened back, top to bottom, one more time and then emailed an MP3 of the song to himself. It was now time for the song and the track to pass the ultimate test—the car test.

Any songwriter/musician in Nashville—or any place, for that matter—will tell you that no matter how nice and expensive your recording equipment and studio are, when you really want to know how your recording and mix sound, there's only one place to listen to it: your car. It's the place where you listen to the most music, where you know how something *should* sound. Bottom line, if it sounds good in your car, then it will sound good anywhere.

Jake walked outside and hopped into the old, trusty Range Rover and cranked the engine. Now this was a 1998 Range Rover, so there was definitely no Bluetooth, just an old cable he could run from his phone to an auxiliary input on the truck's stereo. He plugged in the phone, scrolled through his emails until he found "Keep Running," downloaded it, and hit PLAY. Then he backed up the Rover and headed toward Seventeenth Avenue South. For some reason, Jake always liked to listen to songs while he drove down Music Row. Something about the history of the area mixing with something new. It was as if the atmosphere could imbue a song with some extra pixie dust.

Now with the dull roar of the truck as the only sound, the familiar strains of "Everybody's Talkin'" came ringing out of the

Rover's speakers. Oh, it was so good. But wait . . . it got better. Just when it sounded like the original version of the song, in came the fresh propulsive train beat that Jake had programmed. Soon, there was Jake's voice singing the new song "Keep Running" over the old "Everybody's Talkin'" chord progression. Holy crap, it was amazing! Jake let out a yelp inside the old Rover and couldn't help bopping his head up and down as he stopped for a red light at Seventeenth and Edgehill. He was dancing in his driver's seat like a teenager when something on the sidewalk caught his eye. Jake looked to his left, and there, standing on the sidewalk, smiling and dancing with the beat that must have been blaring out of the truck, were Sir Daniel Smith-Daniels and Misha.

"Oh my god," Jake said aloud as he turned down the stereo and lowered the window. "Ha ha, no one should ever have to see that."

"No, don't stop," said Sir Kid, still dancing. "We love it, and the song sounds amazing! Let it play!"

Jake turned down the track.

"Well, that's embarrassing," Jake said looking up at the still red light. "But hey, I think this song could be a smash."

"It's a bop for sure," said Misha, still dancing in place and laughing. "Is that the one you just wrote with Shane Sawyer?"

"That would be it. And oh, you gotta hear about the flight up to Louisville."

"Ha! I surmise you're referring to Shane's air acrobatics?" Daniel mimicked a plane with his hands flying upside down and doing loop the loops. The light turned green.

Jake started rolling forward but shouted out the window, "Holy crap! You knew he was going to pull that on me?"

"Why, Jake," Misha yelled after the departing truck, "if he tries to kill you, it means he's a fan of your work. It's an honor."

"You're crazy. See ya!"

Jake hit the gas, and he couldn't help but see this moment as a metaphor for what had been happening in his life the past couple of weeks. Everything seemed to suddenly be opening up, moving forward—a huge "Go" sign, if you will. Jake wasn't the kind of person to ascribe anything in his life to a certain event or process, but he couldn't deny that since he'd had that fortuitous lunch with Brice, his life had dramatically changed for the better. His writing, his mood, his health, and most importantly, Jake realized, his relationship with his wife and son. It had all changed—because he had.

As if on cue, his phone rang. It was Sarah.

Jake hit the green button and asked, "Are your ears burning?"

"Ha, are you talking about me?"

"Well, I'm thinking about you. Does that count?

"I think I'll accept that," Sarah said. "So, Mac had a fun idea for dinner."

"Hit me."

"How about we go to Dave & Buster's for some burgers and games?"

Now, ordinarily, going to a family arcade restaurant would be the last thing that Jake would ever want to do. So he knew exactly what he needed to do.

"I think that's a fabulous idea! I can't think of anything I'd rather do tonight than kick both your butts in Skee-Ball."

"It's on, sucka!" Sarah laughed and hung up the phone.

Jake put the phone down and hit PLAY again on "Keep Running."

Damn, this sounds good, he thought and winked to himself in the rearview mirror.

Good work, Jake. We're back!

BRIDGE (*brij*) *n.* provides a contrast to both the verse and the chorus || usually introduces a new chord progression and lyrics (i.e. shakes things up) || often occurs toward the end of a song and reinforces the lyrical message || breaks up the repetition of the song and provides a reset before returning to the final chorus.

Chapter 9

PRACTICE FIVE: *DARE TO BE STUPID*

Saturday morning, bright and early, Jake received a text from Sir Kid asking if he could meet him for lunch at his home south of town. Jake felt a sense of déjà vu. It had been exactly two weeks since he'd received a similar text from Daniel before their first meeting at The Row.

What a difference two weeks makes, thought Jake as he poured himself a cup of French-pressed coffee. *Feels like it's been a year since I met him.*

And while Jake had been slammed since that fateful meeting two weeks ago, he didn't feel worn out. On the contrary, he felt energized. There seemed to be a sense of balance, of peace, that he couldn't quite put his finger on. As Jake took a sip of coffee, he noted that the street address Daniel gave him was unfamiliar, but a quick check on his phone's map app showed Jake that it was south of Nashville, over near Leiper's Fork.

Leiper's Fork was something else. Nestled among the horse farms and rolling green hills of Williamson County twenty miles south of downtown Nashville, Leiper's was a charming hamlet that looked plucked from some other time. There was a general store, a little gas station called Fox & Locke that had nightly live music, Country Boy Cafe, a few antique stores that dotted the quaint two-lane road that ran through town, and that was about it. If you looked up "charming" in the dictionary, there would be a woodblock etching of Leiper's Fork.

That said, you would be wrong to think that it was simple country folk that lived there. Far from it. In the past ten years, the little town had become an enclave for some of the biggest artists in music, not to mention professional athletes who played for the Tennessee Titans and the Nashville Predators. Scattered throughout the surrounding hillsides, music stars like Justin Timberlake, Chris Stapleton, and Tim McGraw made their homes on one-hundred-plus-acre properties. If you were to pop into any store in Leiper's on any given day, you might run into a star athlete from the Titans, *American Picker*'s Mike Wolf, and now, it seemed, billionaire boy-genius, Sir Daniel Smith-Daniels.

The Waze app finally brought Jake to a nondescript mailbox on a small road about half a mile from the center of town. Jake checked Daniel's text again for the street number and looked at the mailbox. This was it. Over the hood of the Rover, a driveway serpentined through a meadow bordered by a rock-lined stream on one side.

"Ah, a babbling brook," Jake said aloud in his best highbred English accent.

He continued for a couple hundred yards, and then the drive began an incline as it entered a strand of trees. It was gorgeous, and not just by accident. The trees, the vegetation along the drive—it had all been planted recently by a very talented landscaper. It looked like he was driving through the middle of Central Park.

When the Rover entered the trees, the driveway began a series of switchbacks, going up a steep incline on the side of a large hill. By the looks of it, Daniel's house was going to be perched all alone on the top of one of the tallest peaks in Williamson County. The Rover did not appreciate the steep climb.

"Come on, baby, don't let me down." Jake stroked the dusty dashboard of the old SUV. "Just a little farther."

As Jake began to round the crest of what he thought was a hill, it quickly became apparent that it was more mountain than hill, and on top of this mountain was one of the most stunning modern homes imaginable.

"Blimey, Sir Daniel," Jake said aloud. "You've outdone yourself."

As he drove slowly on the now flat drive atop the plateau, what unfolded before him was nothing less than the coolest home Jake had ever seen. It was like something out of *Dwell*, but times a thousand. Fusing wood, steel, and stone, the sprawling modern home covered what seemed to be most of the top of the mountain.

Will wonders never cease, Sir Daniel? Jake thought as he pulled into a parking spot on the large parking pad. *Gonna have to write a few more songs before I can buy this beauty.*

Jake grabbed his computer bag and exited the Rover, taking in the meticulous landscaping as he walked up the winding path to the front door. It looked, for the most part, like the space was one story, though a huge two- to three-story structure rose toward the rear of the house. As Jake got closer, the massive front door swung open.

"I see you made it up the hill," Sir Daniel Smith-Daniels said as he stepped out into the early morning sun. "Welcome!"

"Oh, it was touch-and-go with the old Rover for a second," Jake said, as he approached the house. "But we made it before she blew a gasket."

"Ha, and that gasket would've cost you a fortune." Daniel shook Jake's hand and then gave a quick Nashville hug. "I know what a money pit owning an old Rover is. It's endless!"

"Yes, yes, I know. Sarah says I should get rid of it."

"Well, after hearing the songs you've been writing the past couple of weeks," Daniel motioned for Jake to follow him, "I think you'll be able to afford whatever kind of vehicle you want."

"You've heard some of the demos?" Jake asked as they walked into the foyer of the home. It was stunning. Daniel turned around as he walked over a massive *kilim* rug that must have been forty feet long.

"Mate, I've heard the track you wrote with Brit and Misha."

"Yeah? 'Perilous'?"

"Yes, and it's an absolute smash." Daniel turned right off the long foyer, which brought them into a massive open kitchen filled with the latest German appliances, or so Jake guessed by the number of umlauts in the brand names. "Brit sent the track to Ellie Goulding, who's a friend."

"Of course." Jake leaned against the kitchen island, which was impossibly long and topped with smooth black stone.

"Not surprising, huh? Brit runs with everybody, but yes, Ellie loves it and is planning on cutting a vocal on it beginning of next week. I think Brit's going to fly to London to record it himself." Sir Daniel walked over to a restaurant-level espresso machine.

"Whoa, that's amazing," Jake said as he found a bar stool to sit on. "I love her voice."

"It's incredible, and she's coming off a huge single. And she thinks 'Perilous' could be her follow-up. Want an espresso?"

"Uh, yeah. With that news, make it a double!" Jake slapped his hands together. "I've already had some French press, but I may as well go into turbo mode."

"God bless caffeine," Daniel praised as he negotiated the machine. It really looked like some steampunk creation. "Without it, there would be no songs!"

"Amen to that."

Daniel finished making espressos for each of them, and then he led Jake through the house, talking as they walked. It really was like walking through the most incredible interior design store ever. Jake took in the impressive collection of African masks and artwork on the expansive walls.

"So, tell me, Jake," Daniel said as they continued snaking their way through the massive sunlit home, "you've completed four writes—four of the five 'practices,' if you will—of The Method. I'm curious . . . What do you think?"

"First off, I got to get my bearings. My head is spinning from this amazing house."

"When you hire great designers, you get this. I wish I could take credit."

"I'm sure you had something to do with it," Jake said. "But to answer your question, Daniel, honestly, when we met, I really didn't know what to think of the whole Method."

"Sounded a little hocus-pocus-y?"

"Well, yeah. I mean it all sounded a little suspect to a grizzled veteran such as myself." Jake rubbed the stubble on his chin, and Daniel led him through another massive door that opened to a long, platinum-album-filled hallway. Every huge international artist you could imagine was represented. "And truth be told, I wasn't in the greatest place. Just kind of stuck in neutral."

"I get that."

"But I have to say, creative collaboration, filling the well, leaving my comfort zone, and—"

"Changing your attitude," Daniel interjected. "That was Shane's idea, if I'm being honest. I'd always called it, 'A fresh approach,' but I like his whole aviation parlance."

"Yes, that crazy business in the plane, changing my attitude. I thought he was going to kill us. How could you let me go?"

Daniel barked a laugh. "Shane is a lot safer and more accomplished as a pilot than he likes to let on." When they reached the end of the hallway, he placed his fingers on the handle of the large steel door that stood before them. He looked over his shoulder at Jake conspiratorially. "You were in good hands."

"But yes," Jake went on as he stopped with Daniel at the door, "The Method, well, it's really affected how I'm approaching my writing." Jake thought about Sarah and Mac. "And I gotta say, how I'm approaching my personal life too."

Daniel nodded but didn't speak. Jake could see through a skylight in the hallway that they had left the main house and were now in front of the massive structure that he saw looming behind the house when he drove up earlier.

"Jake," Daniel said, "we're about to enter the nerve center of what I do. The brain trust, if you will."

"Oh, cool." *Oh, cool? Very eloquent, Jake.* "Tell me more, Sir Daniel."

"I rarely bring people here, and it is always with a bit of reticence that I do so." Daniel stared at Jake intently as he began turning the door handle. "This truly is where all my deepest intellectual dives have taken place in the past five years. I bulwark this spot. It is hallowed ground."

"Understood," Jake said solemnly and as seriously as he could muster. He imagined he must be going into some massive computer bank or library. "Your secrets are safe with me."

With that, Sir Daniel Smith-Daniels opened the heavy steel door, and he and Jake stepped across the threshold. There before him was a full-sized basketball court.

"Whoa," Jake shouted.

The room—uh, *gymnasium*—had a gleaming parquet floor like the old Boston Gardens and all the requisite painted lines: free throw, three-point, etc. And it was humongous. Throughout the space on the "court" were groupings of furniture, desks, recording equipment, and instruments. Jake instantly thought it was like a much larger and more elaborate version of Sir Daniel's room at The Row building up in Nashville, but of course, with the addition of a basketball court. Along all four walls, massive pieces of artwork hung. Jake thought he recognized a Rothko, a Hockney, and a piece by Keith Haring. And on the far wall, there was what appeared to be the largest chalk board Jake had ever seen. It was covered with writing. Sir Kid had taken a gym and turned it into a massive work-live-play space—like the coolest art installation ever.

"Welcome to the inner sanctum!" Daniel looked like an eager kid despite his twenty-eight years. He walked over to a rolling basketball cart and grabbed a ball. "Play a game of HORSE?"

"Well, why the hell not?" Jake got into it as Daniel passed the ball to him. "But I gotta warn you, Sir Kid. I was an all-state point guard back in high school, and I've been known to shoot the lights out. That's a lot to handle for a limey."

"Oh, trash talking before noon. Brilliant!" Daniel clapped his hands together, but oddly, the room didn't echo like most gyms—far from it. The room was completely dead, acoustically speaking. From the ceiling of the structure hung stunning architectural baffles that somehow made the room almost silent, as if they were in a small carpeted room. The effect was magical.

"Who goes first?" Jake asked.

"Age before beauty." Daniel passed the ball to him. "Your shot."

Jake grabbed it and made an easy layup, which Daniel made, as well. On his next shot, he made a turnaround jumper, which Daniel missed.

"There's an H for you," said Jake as Daniel passed him the ball. "Stings, doesn't it?"

"Ha, it's a long game!" Daniel shot back in his clipped accent.

The game went back and forth, with each player making great shots. Sir Daniel, for his part, kept making trick shot after trick shot. Soon it was H-O-R-S to H-O-R-S.

"Well, ladies and gentlemen, messieurs and madams, we have a proverbial barn burner," Jake said in his best bad English accent as he tried to make a Kareem-style hook shot from the three-point line. It was a beautiful airball.

"That we do, Jake." Daniel grabbed the ball as it bounced off a massive hanging mural that reminded Jake of a Mark Rothko work. "Now it's my turn to put the nail in the coffin."

Daniel dribbled the ball over past the top of the key and past the three-point line. Soon, he was in a grouping of furniture on a large *kilim*—a little sitting area with a few guitars.

Daniel grabbed the ball and stepped onto a Victorian-era-styled sofa. He put one foot on a burled walnut coffee table, so he was straddling the two, with his back turned to the hoop.

"To use your American parlance," Daniel said, laughing. "I call this 'The Couch Potato,' although it is more of a chaise."

Daniel leaned back, limbo-style, so he could see the basket upside down. He rolled the ball in his hands, and then, doing a backwards granny shot, heaved the ball toward the hoop. Jake rolled his eyes and laughed out loud at the silliness of the shot. And then it went in.

Nothing but net.

Daniel hooted, jumping down from the couch. "String music!"

"Holy crap! That is the most ridiculous-looking shot I've ever seen. How in the hell did you make that?" Jake demanded as he got the rebound.

"Why, thank you. Please! Thank you all!" Daniel made a big flourish and bowed. "Your shot, Jake."

It wasn't lost on Jake that he was playing HORSE with a certified genius who was beating him with the dumbest shots he'd ever seen. He dribbled the ball over to the sofa and coffee table, which, upon closer inspection, appeared to be pristine antiques.

"Daniel, I don't know how in the hell you made that shot." Jake gingerly stepped onto the sofa with one foot and the coffee table with the other. He winced at the thought of putting his feet on such gorgeous pieces. "If I don't throw my back out trying to do this, I'll be lucky."

"Embrace the silly, Jake. Let it guide you."

Jake steadied himself with his back to the hoop and leaned over backwards so he could just make out the rim. He turned the ball back and forth in his hands, steadied himself again, then heaved the ball toward the general direction of the hoop.

The ball left his hands, spinning, and made a huge arc towards the basket, then went wide left, and bounced against a mural-covered wall.

"Dang it," Jake said as he hopped off the furniture. "Good game!"

"Why, thank you!" Sir Daniel smiled as he picked up the rolling basketball. "Never underestimate the power of the ridiculous shot."

"Of the *stupidest* shot ever," Jake said. "Really, you had to have practiced that shot."

"Ha! I'll never reveal my secrets, Jake." Daniel dribbled over to the basketball caddy and placed the ball with the others.

"Congratulations, Sir Daniel Smith-Daniels!" Jake clapped his hands in the oddly echo-free gymnasium. "You've taken the trick shot to a whole new level."

"Ah, but what better way to illustrate the fifth and final practice in The Method," Daniel said as he beckoned Jake to follow him to the far end of the gym.

"Wait, huh? Come again?" Jake shook his head a little, perplexed. He continued taking in the amazing room.

"Jake, are you familiar with any of Sir Kenneth Robinson's work?"

"Hmmm, one of your Knights of the Round Table friends? I can't say that I am."

"Ha, yes, he was certainly a more appropriate choice for a knight of the British Realm."

Daniel was leading Jake to the massive chalkboard at the far end of the gym. As they got closer, Jake could see that the board was completely covered with complex-looking formulas. In fact, the whole thing appeared to be one long, insanely complex equation, like something out of *A Beautiful Mind*. The chalkboard was even larger than he thought. Thirty . . . maybe forty feet tall?

"Sir Ken, as he referred to himself, was one of Britain's foremost educators and forward thinkers on the topic of creativity and the relative lack of it in modern education. His ideas challenge the long-standing dogma of what a primary and secondary education should look like." Daniel turned to face Jake with his back to the board.

A lightbulb went off in Jake's head. "Wait, has he done a few TED Talks?"

"Why, yes. Hugely popular ones."

"I've seen him. He's great and funny too." Jake craned his neck upward to see to the top of the chalkboard, and he could tell the chalk formulas on the board seemed to be sealed with some type of lacquer. So this wasn't a working chalk board; it was some kind of art piece.

"Ah, he was more than funny. He was hilarious. Sadly, though, he passed away recently." Daniel followed Jake's eyes up the chalkboard. "The reason I mention Sir Kenneth is because he's the source of one of my all-time favorite quotes."

"Quote away!"

"'If you're not prepared to be wrong, you will never come up with anything original or truly groundbreaking.' Or as the fifth practice in The Method states, and as I just demonstrated in our game of

HORSE"—Daniel lowered his gaze from the chalkboard to Jake's eyes—"dare to be stupid!"

Jake took a beat.

"Wait, what? That's the fifth step of The Method?"

"Correct, Jake, and I believe it is the most important of them all. In a way, the prior four practices pave the way for it." He stepped away from the chalkboard and motioned for Jake to stand next to him. "There's no better way to illustrate this than what you see before you."

"That?" Jake looked up at the incredibly complex-looking long equation.

"That." Daniel put his arms in the air, embracing the scope of the huge chalkboard. "What you're looking at is the chalkboard from my studio in London. This is my formula for Uniform Economic Order Quantity. Without it, I wouldn't be standing here with you today."

"Uh, there's nothing about that that looks stupid, Daniel," he said. "Sorry to disappoint you."

"Oh, but it was, Jake." Daniel pointed to the final equation at the bottom right of the huge frame. "Up until I developed that equation, supply chain economics lacked a formula that would work for all countries and their specific challenges. Imagine, if you will, that every computer had its own unique operating system that didn't interface or work with any other computer. Or what if each musical instrument guitar, piano, what have you, had its own tuning?"

Finally, Jake understood the analogy. "No instrument could play along with any other instrument."

"Ding, ding, ding! Precisely. And I might add that until, oh, one hundred years ago, a 'standard' tuning—440—didn't exist. Can you believe that?"

"Oh, I had no idea," Jake said. "I just assumed there was always a standard tuning."

"Most people, even most musicians, think that, as well. So back to this." He gestured to the formula on the wall.

"The UEOQ?"

"Precisely, ha, yes. So, with no *uniform* EOQ, continents like Africa were shut out of the world's economy. The prevailing thinking was that a uniform EOQ was a fantasy."

"Then you dared to be stupid?" As always, he wasn't quite sure where Daniel was heading.

"Exactly, Jake. I went against everything that I was taught was correct, against the accepted dogma of economics, risked looking like a fool to my colleagues and academia and wrote out a 'stupid' formula that would take into account the deltas, or differences, inherent to a domestic economy. Trust me when I say that until I proved the formula, every leading economist would have said it was a joke! Gibberish!"

"Okay, well, I think I'm starting to get it." Jake was not starting to get it at all.

"Let me frame what I'm saying in songwriting terms." Daniel walked over to a large grouping of plush furniture and plopped down in what looked like a space-age beanbag. "What would you say is Brice Smith's strength as a songwriter?"

"He's an amazing lyricist. Just out-of-the box ideas."

"Yes, but the reason he's a great lyricist is that he has no filter. He throws every idea out into the songwriting session, with no concern for how ridiculous it might sound to his cowriters. He dares to be stupid and doesn't give a damn."

"He does come up with some terrible ideas when he gets going." An understatement, Jake thought.

"Yes, of course, but then out comes that golden nugget of a lyric." Daniel's eyes lit up. "And here's where dare to be stupid builds on the other practices. In creative collaboration, we work in an environment where ideas, no matter how ridiculous they may sound on the surface, are not stigmatized if they're wrong or don't work. You work in an environment—you create a space—where you are encouraged to think outside the box, to be unafraid of looking 'stupid' for proposing an original thought. An environment where no one has second-guessed themselves."

"Like my session with Brit and Misha a couple weeks ago." Jake nodded. "Really, like all my sessions with The Row writers. It's been incredibly freeing. Everyone in the session is so comfortable."

"I love hearing that," he said. "And with Practice Two, filling the well, you are given new and fresh inspiration, tools, and data to draw upon so you can continue to be—"

"As stupid as you wanna be?" Jake was starting to get where Daniel was heading.

"Precisely. And when we leave our comfort zones and find ourselves in a creatively new or uncomfortable position—" Daniel was standing now on the massive coffee table in the center of the sitting area.

"Like wearing a white thong on a float boat?" Jake was in rhythm with him now.

"Yes! When we're off balance and in flux, that's when we're forced to adapt and be creative. Once we get over our embarrassment, of course."

"Daniel, somehow we wrote an amazing song: 'Still Waters,'" Jake said. "I thought the ghastliness of my appearance was going to throw everyone off."

"Oh, I heard the work tape, and so has Miranda Lambert. Apparently, she loves it." Daniel walked over to what looked like a mobile bar with stools by the three-point line.

"Holy crap, for real?" Jake couldn't believe all the action his songs were getting.

"For real, Jake. It's an exceptional song. But let's go back to the fifth practice." Daniel gestured back up to the massive chalkboard. "When you were with Shane and he took you up in the air to demonstrate changing your attitude—"

"Don't remind me. I'll get airsick thinking about it," Jake said, fighting the memory.

"But one of the strategies you discussed for changing your angle of approach, for breaking a creative deadlock, was tackling the songwriting backwards—to reverse engineer a hit song, so to speak." Daniel reached into a cooler and pulled out a couple of Topo Chico waters.

"Yeah, I remember we discussed that. We talked about a Sam Smith song we loved and then broke down those elements to see how it started."

"Exactly. Well, that's what I did here." Daniel looked back up at the chalkboard. "I just wrote out what my ideal Uniform Economic Order Quantity equation would be and then worked backward. And as ridiculous as it seemed at the time, well, it worked, and it brought me here."

"Well, it's pretty amazing."

"I really can't overstate it enough." Daniel took a sip. "Everything I have—the success, the homes, the knighthood, The Row—everything came from daring to be stupid."

"'Everything is impossible until it's done'," Jake said.

"Yes, my favorite Nelson Mandela quote," Daniel said.

"You know, speaking of daring to be stupid . . ." Jake took of sip of the Topo Chico. "Last week, on a lark, practicing contrary action, I might add—"

"Well done."

"Well, I wrote a song with a high school friend's daughter, Brie." Jake searched his memory bank for her last name.

"Turner." Daniel said matter-of-factly.

"Yeah." Jake nodded. "Wait, how do you know her name?"

"Well, if you recall, you allowed The Row access to your writing calendar so we could add your writes in over the past couple of weeks."

"Oh, that's right. Damn, good memory." Jake continued. "But we wrote this song—"

"'Great Day'," Daniel said. "It's an insanely catchy song."

"Okay, now you're scaring me," Jake said.

"I saw Brie perform it on a YouTube video that's gone a bit viral over the past couple of days."

"Wait, huh? How is that possible?"

"Well, earlier this week," he said, "the songwriter Ryan Tedder visited Belmont to teach a songwriting class and listen to songs by several of the students."

"Oh wow." Jake sat upright on the bar stool and remembered that Brie had said they were going to have a special guest coming to visit their class.

"Well, students were going around playing their demos, and someone must have decided to film it. Ryan was giving pointers and critiques to the different songs, nothing exceptional really, but when Brie played 'Great Day,' Ryan was blown away. You must watch his face, his reaction when he's listening."

"Wow . . . again."

"Wow, indeed." Daniel grabbed another Topo Chico from the cooler. "When the song was over, Ryan was speechless, and when he finally spoke, well, he said there was nothing he could offer, that the song was flawless, that what the class had all just heard was a smash."

"Oh my god, that's incredible! Why am I just hearing this now?" Jake spun around on his bar stool.

"Well, you've been busy in the studio." Daniel nodded to Jake.

"Uh, yeah, but the whole reason I brought up the song is that it's an example of daring to be stupid," he said. "Truth be told, I was doing as you instructed, practicing contrary action. Normally I wouldn't have booked a session with an unknown writer, especially when it came through Facebook from a high school friend, but I did."

"Well done."

"Yes, but I went in the session completely carefree and just followed Brie. Instead of trying to be cool, I decided to just be silly, and out came the most stupidly happy song I've ever written with anyone."

"Ha! Jake, I think you need to do that more often."

"You're probably right. But I believe my old publisher, Chuck Lane at MegaMusic, is signing her," Jake said.

"On the contrary, Jake. I signed her to The Row yesterday."

"You scooped her from Chuck?" Jake raised his arms. "Yes!"

"When I saw the YouTube video—which has almost one hundred million views, I might add—I knew I had to sign her. Jake, this silly little song you wrote *is* going to be a smash. Mr. Tedder was correct in his assessment. There is a bidding war heating up to sign

Brie to a record label. By all accounts, this song is going to be huge. Kids are already doing covers of it on TikTok. I suggest you write more with Brie. Her other songs are quite good, but they could definitely use your touch."

"Daniel, this is the craziest, greatest news I've heard in a while." Jake was simply blown away. "I'm going to have to reach out to Brie's dad."

"Cal?" Daniel was yet again scooping Jake with a name.

"You are amazing, Daniel. I'm going to start calling you Nostra-Daniel. Yes, I'm going to reach out to Cal."

"Good man," Daniel said. "And I rather fancy Nostra-Daniel, much more than Sir Kid."

"It is your new title," Jake said in his terrible British accent, holding his water bottle out like a sword. "Hear ye, hear ye, henceforth thou shalt be known throughout all thine realms as Nostra-Daniel—bon vivant, prognosticator, and stupid thinker!"

Daniel laughed and lit up. "I love it! And let me ask if you are willing to have a new title, as well?"

"Uh-oh, bring it." Jake braced himself.

"Jake Stark, would you accept my offer to be an official writer at The Row? With all its accompanying titles and privileges?" Daniel made a flourish with his hand.

"Hey! I passed the test?" Jake knew he was beaming; he had done it. "I finished The Method with flying colors?"

"Jake, we would be honored to have you as a writer at The Row. You're a pleasure to work with and would be an asset to the company," Daniel said, suddenly sincere.

"Thanks, Daniel. I'd be happy to call The Row my new home." Jake stood up and did a little bow.

"Brilliant, but I must correct you on one thing." Daniel stood, as well. "We never *finish* The Method. On the contrary, we must practice it every day. When done correctly, ideally, it becomes a way of life that we never quite master, but continue to strive to do so."

"Ah, I got you and agree," Jake said.

"As a great man once said, 'Progress, not perfection.'" Daniel raised his Topo Chico to Jake. "And it is only by practicing The Method on a daily basis that we can not only *have* success—"

"But *keep* success," Jake interjected.

"Bingo, Jake," Daniel exclaimed out as their bottles clinked.

Just then there came a bit of a commotion from the far end of the gymnasium where Jake and Daniel had entered earlier. It sounded like it was coming from the platinum-album-lined hallway that connected the house to the gym. It was the unmistakable sound of a group of people coming their way.

"Sounds like we have some company." Daniel raised an eyebrow to Jake as he spun around on the stool to face the far end of the court.

"A lot of company." Jake got up from the stool as Daniel began to walk toward the noise at the far end of the gym.

The sound grew louder, and then the massive steel door at the end of the gym burst open. In quick succession, out came all The Row writers Jake had worked with over the past two weeks: Brit, Misha, Kate, Dara, Tom, Dan, Shane, and at the back of the crowd, Brice Smith, the man who started all of it a couple of weeks ago.

"Holy crap, what a sight!" Jake said.

And just when he thought the parade of people had ended, Sarah and Mac emerged from the hallway.

"Oh my god, hey, you guys." Jake was elated.

"Let's play some ball," shouted Tom and Dan.

"Welcome, everybody," Daniel shouted as he began embracing each person as they came in. "Time to get our brunch on! Follow me."

Jake greeted everyone with high fives and handshakes, and then came to Sarah and Mac, both beaming, Sarah wearing the casual but clingy black-and-white outfit she knew he loved.

"Hey! I'm so happy you're here." Jake hugged his family. "So wait, Sarah, you knew when I left this morning you were coming to meet me here?"

"Yeah, guilty," she said. "Daniel wanted it to be a surprise."

"Well, it's a good one." Jake took a step back and looked at Mac.

"Dad, this house and gym . . . Insane." Mac caught a pass from Dan Walker. "Three-pointer, everyone!"

The ball went up and in—nothing but net.

"He drains it, ladies and gents," Dan shouted with his arms raised.

The group seemed to know where they were going as they headed toward a double door on the side of the gym directly below what looked like a massive David Hockney painting.

"Jake, we have a tradition at The Row," Daniel said as he and Dara pushed open the double doors. "First Saturday of every month, weather permitting, we have brunch out by the pool, so here we are."

The doors to the gym opened, and the group was greeted by a burst of sunlight. When Jake's eyes adjusted, he took in an incredible manicured backyard and stunning pool with a waterfall and an impossibly high diving board.

"Dad, there's a freaking waterfall," Mac said, and he ran out to investigate.

It was just after 11:00 a.m. and an already warm May day in Middle Tennessee. Mac was wearing swim trunks and barely took time to slow down as he pulled off his shoes and shirt and dove headfirst into the deep end of the pool.

"Babe, can you believe all this?" Jake looked at Sarah as they walked over to a large buffet with several cooks and servers milling about. "I told you the past couple of weeks were an experience."

"Right? I'm starting to see what you mean." Sarah's eyes lit up.

"Well, Daniel made it official." Jake grabbed a plate. "He wants me to be a writer at The Row."

"Yay, that's amazing," Sarah said and looked around the yard. "From the little time I've spent with everyone this morning, it seems like a great group of people. And everyone seems to be on a roll."

"Right? Yeah, it's pretty amazing company," Jake said and dished out some huevos rancheros onto his plate.

"Did you guys talk specifics about the deal?" Sarah was always the business-minded practical one in their marriage.

"Not yet," Jake said.

Just then, Brice walked up.

"So, what do you think, Jake?" Brice asked as he grabbed a plate. "Pretty crazy couple of weeks, huh?"

"Yeah, it's been a helluva couple amazing weeks, and I've got you to thank for it."

"Ah, Jake, I'm such a fan of your work." Brice followed Jake and Sarah over to the long table where everyone was gathering. "And I knew you would click with everyone here. *And* Daniel was already a fan of yours, as well."

"Okay, boys, enough talk." Sarah put a napkin in her lap. "Let's chow!"

For the next thirty minutes or so, the large group dug into the amazing brunch spread that Daniel had provided the writers. A steady stream of new songs from The Row writers played from speakers discretely hidden around the pool and backyard area. After everyone seemed to have finished their food, Daniel stood up at the end of the long rectangular table and tapped his champagne flute with his spoon.

"Excuse me, everyone, I'd like to propose a toast." Daniel held his glass aloft. "Now, it isn't an easy task to add a new writer to our incredible roster. Several weeks ago, Brice mentioned an old friend of his might soon be available, and well, when he said that person was none other than Jake Stark, I knew we had to have his talents here at our little company."

"Hear, hear!" Shane shouted with his glass aloft.

"And Brice's instinct and my enthusiasm were only confirmed by the feedback and the songs that you all and Jake have written over the past couple of weeks. So with that said, please, everyone join me in welcoming the illustrious Jake Stark to The Row family!"

The table erupted in bravos and congratulations as everyone took sips and nodded in Jake and Sarah's direction. Mac came up to the table dripping with water.

"Come on, Dad, let's see you jump off that," Mac shouted as he pointed to the high dive at the end of the pool. The whole table hopped on board, taunting Jake. Daniel spoke up over the din.

"Looks like you'll have to take the plunge, Jake," Daniel called as he poured himself another glass of champagne.

"Oh, sorry, no bathing suit," Jake said. "And Dara, don't even think about offering me one!"

"Th-th-th-th-th-thong," Dan and Tom Walker chimed in in perfect harmony. Jake raised his fist in the air at them.

"Oh my god, I can't think of it so soon after eating." Dara put her hand over her mouth, but it didn't do much to conceal her laughter.

"Well, Jake," Sarah said as she reached into the bag sitting next to her chair. "I decided to pack one of your suits, just in case . . ."

"Oh man, why do I feel like I'm being set up," Jake said, as Sarah handed him a pair of surf shorts.

"Go, Jake! Make haste!" Daniel shouted as the rest of the table began hooting and hollering.

Five minutes later, Jake found himself climbing up the ridiculously tall ladder to the top of the diving board. Once again, he swallowed down his fear of heights and walked out onto the platform. It must have been forty or fifty feet in the air. He looked down and took in the view. By now, most everyone had jumped into the pool, and they were swimming or floating on rafts.

Jake gulped as cheers rose from below.

He could see Sarah and Mac along with everyone else looking up and clapping.

"I don't want to do this," Jake shouted as he began to jump lightly up and down on the end of the board. He could hear a chant of "Jake, Jake, Jake" rising from below.

And then, right in that moment, he knew he was right where he should be—in that uncomfortable position, out of his comfort zone, surrounded by friends and his new team, not to mention the loves of his life, Sarah and Mac. He began to bounce higher.

Here's to changing my attitude, Jake couldn't help but think.

"Jake," Daniel shouted over the clamor, "remember what I said to you when we first had breakfast? Leap—"

"Leap," Jake shouted back as he jumped higher, bouncing up and down on the board fifty feet up in the air, "and the net will appear!"

And with that, Jake Stark leapt off the board and into a new lease on life, career, love . . . and the waiting pool below.

RULES FOR DARING TO BE STUPID

1. You will never come up with anything truly groundbreaking unless you're prepared to be wrong.

2. In a creative endeavor, never second-guess yourself.

3. Create an environment where big, out-of-the-box thinking is encouraged, and failure is not stigmatized.

4. We are all in a business of "no"; it just takes one "yes" to begin being successful.

5. Remove the filter, have fun, and dare to be stupid.

Chapter 10

THE GREATEST SONG

Over the next couple of weeks, Jake dove into his writing sessions, most of which were booked by Misha at The Row, but Jake booked a few on his own, as well. At every session, there was a new spark, a new enthusiasm for writing that he hadn't felt in years. Driving home one day, he realized what it was—it was the feeling that his best songs, his biggest successes, still lay in front of him. By embracing the five practices of The Method in some way or another on a daily basis, Jake had felt his whole creative world just open up, and he was on a songwriting roll.

His relationship with Sarah and Mac was different. Sarah had always understood that their relationship would not be "normal" by most definitions because of his career, and she had seldom complained. That didn't mean she was happy; he understood that now. It meant she loved him, and she was honoring her commitment to him. Now, though, he could honor his to her. By "collaborating" with his family, listening, and trying fresh approaches to the everyday tasks of life, Jake was in a better place with Sarah than he'd been in years. And by practicing contrary action with Mac, not doing or saying the first thing that popped into his head when dealing with his son, well, they started being friends again and hanging out with each other more around the house. Jake started feeling a sense of peace that had eluded him for most of his life.

During this time, Jake's lawyer, Kent Davis, was also doing the normal back-and-forth with business affairs from The Row, hammering out the terms of the deal with his new company. Normally, this was a time when all the goodwill of the courtship often went out the window, when the lawyers start going back and forth on terms, but Kent kept expressing to Jake how amenable and easy dealing with The Row's team had been thus far. In fact, it appeared that execution copies were ready to sign. Not long after hearing this, Jake received one of Sir Kid's famous early-morning texts inviting him over to The Row to ink the deal on the following Friday. When the morning rolled around, Jake found himself once again driving down Music Row in the old Range Rover. The vehicle sounded particularly bad that morning.

C'mon, old girl. Jake patted the aged dashboard of the truck. *Hang on. We've got each other for a little while longer.*

In negotiating the impending publishing deal, Jake had the option to take a big cash advance against future royalties or take a very low advance in exchange for better terms. It was really a choice between grabbing the cash or betting on himself to bring in the money with his new songs. Given where he was creatively, now equipped with the practices of The Method *and* the new batch of songs he'd written over the past month, Jake had decided on the latter and negotiated for a low advance and better terms—he'd keep more of his royalties and give The Row a smaller percentage. All of this meant, though, that for the time being, Jake would still be driving around the beat-up old Range Rover.

As Jake approached the gleaming modern structure of The Row, which stood out so starkly amongst its neighbors, he couldn't help but think how far he'd come since his first visit.

Turning into the drive, he slowly pulled up to the sleek pylon rising up from the concrete like a tulip. And once again, before he could press a call button, Misha's voice greeted him with her warm British accent.

"Good morning, Jake Stark!" She was as bright as ever.

"Misha, good morning," Jake said, turning his face toward the building. "How do you know it's me before I even press the button?"

"Oh, Jake, you're dealing with Sir Daniel Smith-Daniels." Misha lowered her voice. "There's not only face recognition software, but car recognition software, as well. Truth be told, though, I saw you pulling up from the window."

"Ha! Old school. Okay, let me in. I'm ready to get down to business," Jake said as the seamless wall of The Row's garage opened up.

"See you shortly," said Misha as Jake drove the Rover forward into the parking area.

He approached the dark glass doors that opened into the foyer, and just like the first time he came to The Row, there was Sir Daniel Smith-Daniels waiting to greet him.

"Ladies and gentlemen, I give you the one, the only, Jake Stark!" Daniel sounded like a British P. T. Barnum. "Good morning."

"Good morning, sir." Jake gave Daniel a fist bump. "What a fine morning it is. Perfect spring weather."

"Ah yes, the weather is auspicious indeed, Jake." Daniel turned and walked into the waiting elevator. "It bodes well for our new partnership."

"Right? Time to make it official." Jake entered the elevator and turned to face the modern foyer. "You know, the first time I was in this elevator, I shared it with Ed Sheeran."

"Ah, that sounds about right. He came to see me the day you wrote with Brit and Misha. We have to get you two together."

"Good memory, Daniel," Jake said as the doors opened to the fifth floor. "And yes, I'll see if I can find some time in my calendar to squeeze Ed in."

"And speaking of Misha," Daniel stepped out of the elevator, "here she is."

"What a wonderfully good morning," Misha sang as she gave Daniel a quick hug and then did the same with Jake. "It's great to see you both, but I'm just on my way out for the weekend. Everything's set up out in the garden, though."

After saying their goodbyes, Jake and Daniel stepped out onto the pea gravel walkway, and Jake was temporarily blinded by the brilliant Nashville sunshine. It was shaping up to be a gorgeous day.

Jake took a seat at the same table he'd occupied only a few weeks before under such different circumstances, and once they were both seated, Daniel cleared his throat.

"Jake, I want you to know what a dream come true it is for me that you're making your new home here at The Row." Daniel grabbed the closing documents from the side of the table. "I couldn't be prouder and more honored to have you as part of our family."

Just then, a waiter appeared from behind the tall boxwoods with a bottle of Dom Perignon.

"Sir Daniel, breaking out the good stuff."

"Jake, we have to celebrate. This is a momentous occasion," Daniel said. "But first, let's make it official."

"Let's go," Jake said.

Daniel laid out the short stack of publishing documents so that the signing pages were visible and facing Jake. At the same time, the waiter handed both Jake and Daniel The Row-inscribed Mont Blanc pens.

"You first, Daniel." Jake pointed his pen at Sir Kid.

"My pleasure." Daniel signed the documents in four different places. "Now your turn."

"The pleasure is mine." Jake signed the documents, stacked the papers, and pushed them back to Daniel.

Daniel extended his hand to Jake. "Welcome to The Row."

As they shook hands, the waiter popped the champagne and poured each of them a glass in tall crystal flutes.

"Here's to a brilliant partnership full of collaboration, filling the well—" Daniel stood.

"—Leaving your comfort zone, changing your attitude—" Jake followed suit, standing up.

"—And the most important practice of all . . ." Daniel interjected.

"Daring to be stupid," Jake said as they toasted the flutes and drank the champagne.

"Woo-hoo!" Jake said. "Let's do this."

"Congratulations," Daniel shouted.

"Congratulations to you too," Jake shouted right back.

The waiter poured more champagne in the flutes, and they both took sips. Then Daniel began walking and motioned for Jake to follow him on a pea gravel path that Jake had not seen earlier.

"Follow me, Jake. I have something to show you." Daniel looked over his shoulder. "Oh, and one other thing, and it's important. At The Row, we sing it forward."

"What's that exactly?" Jake asked as he fell in line behind Daniel.

"Just as Brice thought you would be a good fit and reached out to you about The Row . . ." Daniel disappeared around a turn in the path. "You must now find someone you believe would be an excellent fit, as well. We call it sing it forward because we don't keep The Method as a secret; we share it."

"I get it, like pay it forward."

"That's it exactly," Daniel said as they continued to walk.

"I think it's a great idea. I can think of a couple of people and will whittle it down from there."

"Good man," said Daniel as he made another sharp turn along the serpentine path.

As Jake walked after Daniel, he got a sense of just how big The Row's building was. The path wound through boxwoods, bougainvillea, marigolds, and blooming foxglove. It seemed almost endless, especially considering they were on top of a building on Music Row. At last they came to the end of the path, which opened to a circular area bounded by vine-covered iron lattice work. On the floor of the area, framed by more pea gravel, was a round pattern of inscribed flagstones. It looked like a daisy with the petals radiating around the center. It was almost silent in the space. The whole effect was magical.

"Whoa, Daniel, this is something else." Jake turned around, taking it in. "I feel like we've stepped into another world. I can't hear the street, the cars, birds . . ."

"Ah, that's by design." Daniel put his finger to his temple. "I wanted this hideaway—this cloister, if you will—to be acoustically silent, sonically out of phase with the surrounding environment. It needed to be a meditative space."

"For a meditative state?"

"Ah yes, precisely." Daniel turned around to face Jake. "I needed it to be a place to focus inward with no outside distraction, a place to foster mindfulness."

"I think you've been successful." Jake lowered his voice. "It's perfect."

Sir Daniel Smith-Daniels nodded silently, raised an eyebrow, and took a sip of his champagne as he looked down at the inscribed flagstone. One by one, he regarded the text on each of the five petals that radiated around the round center stone where he and Jake stood.

"Jake, when we first met here at The Row five weeks ago, almost to the day, you told me that you wanted to write the greatest song ever. I'm curious, have you finished it?"

"Oh, ha, yes, *that* . . . The greatest song ever. Well . . . hmm. I can say with the utmost certainty that for the first time in my life, with The Method under my belt, I feel like I might just be equipped to write it." Jake spoke as he read the inscriptions on the five flagstones that surrounded him. There were five different phrases carved into the stones: THE INTRO, THE VERSE, THE CHORUS, THE BRIDGE, and THE CODA. The center stone, where Jake and Daniel stood, was blank.

"Well, Jake, you've written some amazing songs over the past several weeks." Daniel looked down at the stones. "I would even dare to call them brilliant, and you already have some bona fide superstar artists about to cut them. Miranda, Ellie . . ."

"I'm still blown away by how fast that has all gone down," he said. "Just crazy."

"And let us not forget 'Great Day.'" Daniel looked at Jake. "Since we last saw each other two weeks ago, the video I told you about with Brie and Ryan Tedder, it's gone from 100 million views to 250 million views."

"That's insane!" Jake said.

"She's doing a proper recording of the song now, with Ryan producing, and will probably be signing with Warner Brothers records by next week."

"What the—" Jake was nearly speechless.

"Jake, it's going to be a smash. Congratulations in advance."

"It's nuts. I didn't think twice about the song when we wrote it. Talk about daring to be stupid." Jake put his hand to his head.

"It's amazing what we create when we're giving ourselves all the tools we need to have success." Daniel eyed Jake.

"Uh, Sir Kid, I think you meant to say, 'The tools we need to *keep* success.'" Jake was quite proud of himself.

"Aha! You've been listening." Daniel clinked champagne glasses with him. "So back to my question. The songs you've written recently are amazing, and the Brie Turner song, by all accounts, is going to do huge things. Think one of those might be the greatest song ever?"

"I get what you're saying," Jake said. "No, yes, I mean, I love those songs, but is it my best song, the elusive 'best song' out there? The greatest song ever? I don't know. Maybe the greatest song ever is something that's always beyond the horizon, just out of reach, the thing that keeps you going," Jake spoke in the silence of the space.

"Or perhaps it's something different," Daniel looked down again at the radiating circle of flagstones. He waited a beat. "You know, it's funny. You can look at life like a song." Daniel pointed to the flagstone inscribed with THE INTRO. "Take the intro, for example."

"I'm listening."

"When we are born, our song starts. It's a blank sheet of music waiting to be written." Daniel spoke intently. "The melody, the harmony, the key, the meter, the rhythm, the five characteristics of a song that begin with the intro are all up to us. Everyone's intro— what it will be, what it will sound like—is a result of their environment, where and what they are born into, but it quickly becomes up to us. It will be unique, and it will join with the billions of other songs in the world."

Daniel rotated slightly to face THE VERSE flagstone.

"As we grow up, as we get older, we write the verses of our lives, and each verse will be different with each passing year. Verse one might be your childhood. Verse two, when you fell in love for the first time. Verse three, when you went off to university . . ."

"Verse four, when you have your first child." Jake thought of Mac.

"Yes, precisely. And everyone's verses will be different. Some will be happy, sad, joyful, angry, or even silly. Some lives will have only a few verses, and some will have an infinite number. And the number has no bearing on the quality of the life, the quality of the song, because, as we both know, some of the best songs are the shortest. The point is, the verses in everyone's songs are unique to them."

"Truth," Jake said.

"And here we have the chorus." Daniel looked up at Jake and then down again to the flagstones. "The chorus is the theme of our life that will be repeated over and over again. It is the thread that ties all our verses together. And it is ever evolving, deepening, and growing as we get older, as we mature. And it is incumbent on us as creators, as humans, to strive to make our theme, our chorus, something that—when it is repeated or retold—draws in others who want to hear it over and over again."

"That person you want to be around. The person you want to work with." Jake now understood where Daniel was going. "The person you want to be in a relationship with."

"And the bridge," Daniel said, "or as we call it in England, the 'middle eight.' The bridge is the musical or melodic interlude that connects us to the final chorus, and while the chorus is the main theme of the song, the bridge is the break from it. In terms of our lives, the bridge represents the great challenges, the roadblocks that we all confront and must overcome if we are to survive, like financial or health crises. We must draw upon the experiences in our verses and chorus, the tools that they have given us to navigate the waters successfully, so we can sing our chorus again. And then our final chorus."

"I've heard it said," Jake said softly, still taken by the silence of the space where they were, "that when we look back upon our lives, every crisis or major challenge will be seen not as a roadblock but as a jumping off point or an *opportunity* to do something in our lives. I like to think of the bridge as that."

"Precisely, Jake." Daniel turned to the last flagstone. "And here we have the fifth part of the song: the coda, or the outro. This is the ending of the song, the ending of the life, and every good song and life has an ending. Our whole life is a process of writing and rewriting our song, and the goal of a truly fulfilled life is that when we get to the end of it, when we get to the end of our song, others will want to hear it again and again because what we have created for the world will be beautiful. It will be a work of art."

As Jake listened to Daniel, the past five weeks played over in his mind: the day he was let go from his old publisher, the day he met Brice for lunch, the day he met Daniel Smith-Daniels for the first time, and so on and so on. As he stood in the magical space with Daniel, everything began to make sense. An epiphany blossomed in Jake Stark's mind. He looked down at the center round stone where he stood with Daniel, the stone that had no inscriptions whatsoever.

"I understand, Daniel," he said. "The greatest song. It's me, isn't it?"

"Ah, you see now, don't you?" Daniel said and smiled.

"I do, and the reason that we're standing on this blank stone is because we, none of us, are ever finished writing the song of our life."

"And with The Method—" Daniel began.

"—And with The Method, we're given the tools to help make the song of our lives," Jake said and paused as he realized the impact of it. "The greatest song."

CODA (*kō-də*) *n.* the song's great ending 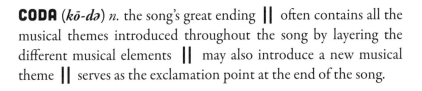 often contains all the musical themes introduced throughout the song by layering the different musical elements ‖ may also introduce a new musical theme ‖ serves as the exclamation point at the end of the song.

EXAMPLE SONG: In "Hey Jude" by The Beatles, the *na na na nas* introduce the coda

Chapter 11

SING IT FORWARD

Jake Stark, husband, father, *and* hit songwriter, walked through the expansive living room of the beachfront home in the exclusive Florida panhandle enclave of Alys Beach. His current single with the Colton Brothers played through the Sonos speaker system in the house, and Jake remembered back to that day when Chuck hadn't picked up his option, and Garrett Colton had mistaken him for a runner at Ocean Way Studios—and asked him to stock the refrigerator, no less.

He had been coming down to this area for years, but never to Alys Beach and never to a house like this. He couldn't even begin to fathom how much a place like this would cost, but if there was anyone who could afford it and then some, well, that would be Sir Daniel Smith-Daniels. Daniel had offered it to Jake and the family for the week, and who was Jake to turn him down?

Jake walked lazily through the living room filled with sleek furniture, and the oh-so-familiar strains of the opening guitar riff from "Everybody's Talkin'" followed the Colton Brothers track. But it wasn't Harry Nilsson's original version. It was Tim McGraw's current number-one country song "Keep Running," written by Jake Stark and Shane Sawyer. Jake had produced the track, as well. He felt himself smile as he remembered going up in that flying death-trap with Shane.

Change your attitude, Jake thought to himself. *I don't care if it got me a hit song or not, I'm never going up with that madman again.*

As he exited the stunning third-floor living room, he walked out onto the balcony that looked down on the powdered sugar white sand and clear blue water of the Gulf of Mexico. It was around 5:00 p.m., and the sun was bouncing off the water as it made its imminent descent over the horizon. Jake bellied up to the railing, and he could see Sarah under an umbrella, reading a book. Just beyond her, Mac was throwing the football with a friend he had brought down with them for the week. They were the only people on the beach. It was a gorgeous vista.

It had been just a year since Jake had signed his deal with The Row, and so much had changed in his life. The biggest thing, the most satisfying thing, was what he was currently staring at: his family and his relationship with Sarah and Mac. Once Jake had met Daniel and started practicing the principles of The Method, not only did his songwriting career take off again, but his career as a father and husband took off, as well. And truth be told, it might've been for the first time. If Jake was being honest with himself, before The Method, he had never been a great family man; he had never been a great husband. He had tried, of course, but he had always come up short somehow.

Once he began collaborating and listening to his family instead of trying to control everything, once he changed his attitude and began approaching the challenges and rewards of a family in different ways, once he took a step back, had fun, and dared to be stupid sometimes—well, that's when life had really gotten sweet.

Oh, and the songwriting career? Well, it was off the charts. Or on the charts, really—the *top* of the charts. Starting with the songs Jake had cowritten in those first two weeks, the past year had been a blur of hits and career highs, and just as Daniel had predicted, "Great Day" turned out to be a certified smash for Brie Turner. The single had hit the radio in June, after it was already a viral sensation on TikTok, and had lit up the charts. The fact that it was the song Apple used to launch the new iPhone didn't hurt either. "Great

Day" was still in the Top 100 in most parts of the world, and the album was currently Top 20. It wasn't buy-a-three-story-right-on-the-beach-house-with-an-elevator-like-Sir-Daniel-Smith-Daniels-level money, but it was allowing Jake to build a house three blocks away from the beach. Not too shabby.

"Perilous," the song Jake had written with Brit and Misha during that first session at The Row, had been a smash for Ellie Goulding, and "Still Waters" had done well for Miranda Lambert, as well. Now, not every song he had written had been a hit or even gotten cut for that matter—that was the game for every songwriter in Nashville, hit songwriters included. The difference now, though, was that by practicing The Method, Jake had exponentially increased his chances of having cuts and hits.

Jake closed his eyes, took in a long, deep breath of the warm gulf air, and brought up songwriting friend Hugh Payne in his phone contacts. It had been a while since they had spoken. Hugh was an incredible songwriting and producing talent who'd had a crazy string of hits for other artists in pop and country about five years ago, at the tender age of twenty-three. The success, whether it was the money or the lifestyle, seemed to have gotten in the way of what had gotten him there in the first place—the songs—and now at twenty-eight, Hugh was a writer without a publishing deal. It sounded more than a little familiar to Jake Stark. Anyhow, Jake had texted Hugh the previous night about hopping on the phone in the evening, and Hugh had seemed only too happy to talk. The phone rang a few times, and then Hugh answered.

"Hello, what's up, Jake?" Hugh answered with his unmistakable Orange County surfer accent.

"Hey, man, I am all good," Jake said, closing his eyes again as he turned his face towards the setting sun. The warmth felt soothing. "How about you?"

"You know, just kicking it, hustling in this songwriting game. Dealing with the lameness of this business and its love of crappy songs."

"Careful, I've built a career on those crappy songs!" He heard a familiar tone in Hugh's voice, a tone that sounded like Jake himself just a little over a year ago.

"Dude, are you kidding? You're on fire across the board. 'Still Waters' is number one right now, right? And jeesh, 'Great Day' is a phenomenon. I can't get away from it!"

"It's crazy, Hugh. And 'Great Day' took about a minute to write."

"Well, next time you got some fire like that in your head, give your boy Hugh a call." His laugh sounded forced.

"Well, hey, man, that's why I'm calling. I hear you're between publishing deals."

"Yeah, man, it's a bunch of bull. Sony didn't want to re-up. It would have been a huge advance they had to give me in order to extend the deal," Hugh said. "I get it, I guess. But yes, I'm currently a free agent. What you thinking?"

"Well, I'm over here at The Row."

"Oh yeah, you're a Knight of the Round Table of Sir what's-his-name," Hugh laughed.

"Yep, Sir Daniel Smith-Daniels. I know, it's crazy he's a knight, but it's the real deal." Jake still shook his head at the improbability of it all.

"You guys are on fire, I'll give you that."

"Well, listen, I'm down here in Florida on vacation, but when I get back next week, how about we grab lunch or something, and I can tell you more about all of it," Jake said as he looked down at his family on the beach.

"I'd like that, Jake," Hugh said. "To be honest, I need a little something different."

"Good to hear. I might just have what you're looking for over at The Row."

"Bring it, son! Let's make us some hits," Hugh said in a singsong voice.

"Right, hits and then some," Jake said. "Okay, I'll hit you on Monday, and we can figure out where we'll hook up."

"I love it. Sounds good." Hugh's voice was a bit more restrained. "And thanks for calling, Jake. I needed some good news."

"Brother, my pleasure. Just singing it forward," Jake said. "Bye, Hugh."

Hugh chuckled softly. "Okay, man, later." The line went dead.

Jake put the phone on the railing of the expansive balcony and once again took in the sun as it began to touch the horizon. He thought about the past year and the ocean of change in his life. Who could have imagined it would all start with a dinner with Brice Smith at Taco Amigo?

Life is crazy. Crazy and beautiful. A wave of gratitude washed over him as he opened his eyes to see an actual wave crashing on the perfect beach scene below.

Then, in that moment, everything seemed to grow quiet: the music inside the house, the sound of the breeze, the random calls of seagulls. There, in that perfect quiet, Jake felt and heard something else. It was a pulse of something, a different kind of music, a beat, a perfect rhythm, but it wasn't coming from a speaker or something around him. It was coming from the inside, somewhere inside Jake's head or his heart, he didn't know which, but he knew what it was—a tune that was unmistakably his, perfectly pure and amazing. It was the sound of his life, his story, playing in perfect rhythm and harmony.

Ah, there you are, Jake thought. *You were there all along, my little smash. I just had to open the doors to let you be heard.*

It was The Greatest Song Ever, because it was the song of Jake Stark, and it filled the songwriter—yep, the *hit* songwriter—with a happiness and sense of peace that had only grown in him over the past year. The sun was dipping even further now on the sublime spring horizon, and Jake just had to smile at the beauty of it all.

His cell phone buzzed, and he looked down at the screen.

A text from Sarah.

Yo, get your butt down here and watch this amazing sunset with me. ;)

Coming, ma'am!!!

And for once, he did what he was told.

ACKNOWLEDGMENTS

The germ of this book was born on that fateful late night in New Orleans when I ran into Brady Wood, and he asked me to speak a few months later in Dallas. So, thank you, Brady, for the opportunity that would eventually lead to *The Greatest Song* being written. Oh, and a big shout out to the world-wide pandemic that would prevent me from touring and speaking and allow me to finish this not-so-weighty tome.

I have been blessed throughout all the twists and turns and ups and downs in my life and career to have been surrounded by amazing people: educators, coaches, bandmates, managers, agents, songwriting collaborators, producers, accountants, lawyers, publishers, sponsors, and friends who each, in their own way, have mentored me and have their fingerprints throughout the pages of this book. Thank you.

To all the fans and supporters who have stood in line, come to the shows, sung along, bought the T-shirts and albums, and streamed the music for over thirty years: thank you, because none of this would have been possible without you.

High praise to all the fine folks at Brown Books and their belief in this project. Big props to my developmental editor, Bonnie Hearn Hill, who encouraged and inspired me to make *The Greatest Song* the best it could be. Megan Reinhardt, thanks so much for the rad artwork for the book. You always blow me away.

The biggest shout-out has to go to my beautiful family. You are the reason for everything I do. My love, Erica; my sons, Max, Graham, and Harrison; my mom, Linda; and my brother, Russ—you all inspire me and keep me moving. Thank you all for everything. I love you.

ABOUT THE AUTHOR

Kevin Griffin is an award-winning songwriter, producer, and performer whose songs have sold in excess of thirty million copies and been streamed over a billion times. He is best known as the singer and founding member of the platinum-selling rock band, Better Than Ezra. He has written numerous #1's and had songs performed by artists such as Taylor Swift, Train, Sugarland, Dierks Bentley, Christina Perri, Hunter Hayes, James Blunt, and many more. He is a co-founder and partner in Pilgrimage Music & Cultural Festival located in Franklin, Tennessee, and has served as a writer-in-residence at NYU's Clive Davis School of Music. Griffin lectures internationally on creativity to groups and companies ranging from Live Nation, Google, Spotify, and Disney to Nike, YPO/WPO and Salesforce. He lives with his family in Franklin, Tennessee.